the Weekend Crafter®

Wirework

the Weekend Crafter®

Wirework

20 Wonderful Wire Projects to Coil, Bend, Twist & Stitch

ELLEN WIESKE

A Division of Sterling Publishing Co., Inc.
New York

This book is dedicated to all of the people who believed in my investigation and teaching of wirework. Thank you all for your support and interest. And to my parents and Carole Ann who always give encouragement.

EDITOR:
MARCIANNE MILLER

ART DIRECTOR & PRODUCTION:
CELIA NARANJO

TOM METCALF

PHOTOGRAPHY:
EVAN BRACKEN
(project photos)
RICHARD HASSELBERG
(how-to photos)

ILLUSTRATIONS:
ORRIN LUNDGREN

EDITORIAL ASSISTANT:
RAIN NEWCOMB

PRODUCTION ASSISTANCE:
HANNES CHAREN
MEGAN KIRBY

PROOFREADER:
CHRIS RICH

Library of Congress Cataloging-in-Publication Data

Wieske, Ellen
The weekend crafter : Wirework : 20 wonderful wire projects to coil, bend, twist & stitch / by Ellen Wieske
p. cm
Includes index
ISBN 1-57990-190-5 (pbk.)
1. Wire craft. I. Title

TT214.3 .W54 2001

2001029119

10 9 8 7 6 5 4 3 2

Published by Lark Books, a division of
Sterling Publishing Co., Inc.
387 Park Avenue South, New York, N.Y. 10016

First Paperback Edition 2001

Distributed in Canada by Sterling Publishing,
c/o Canadian Manda Group, One Atlantic Ave., Suite 105
Toronto, Ontario, Canada M6K 3E7

Distributed in the U.K. by Guild of Master Craftsman Publications Ltd.
Castle Place, 166 High Street, Lewes, East Sussex, England BN7 1XU
Tel: (+ 44) 1273 477374, Fax: (+ 44) 1273 478606
Email: pubs@thegmcgroup.com, Web: www.gmcpublications.com

Distributed in Australia by Capricorn Link (Australia) Pty Ltd.
P.O. Box 704, Windsor, NSW 2756 Australia

If you have questions or comments about this book, please contact:
Lark Books
67 Broadway
Asheville, NC 28801
(828) 253-0467

Printed in China

ISBN 1-57990-190-5

CONTENTS

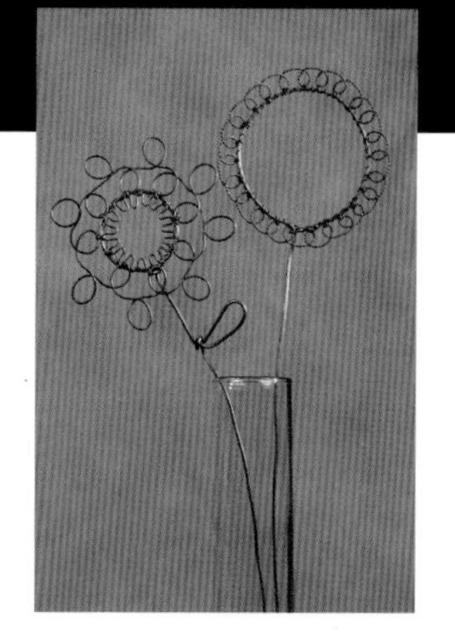

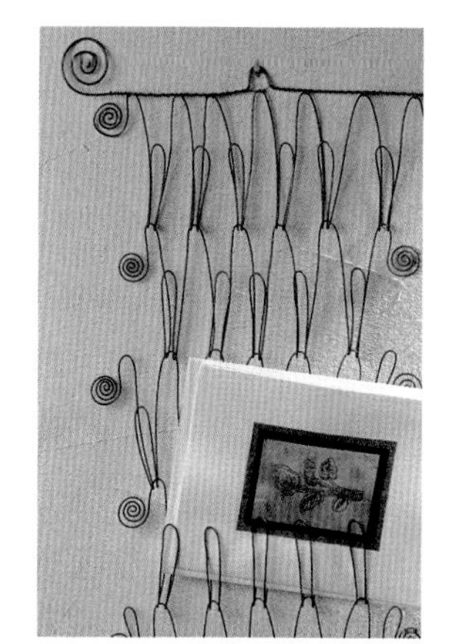

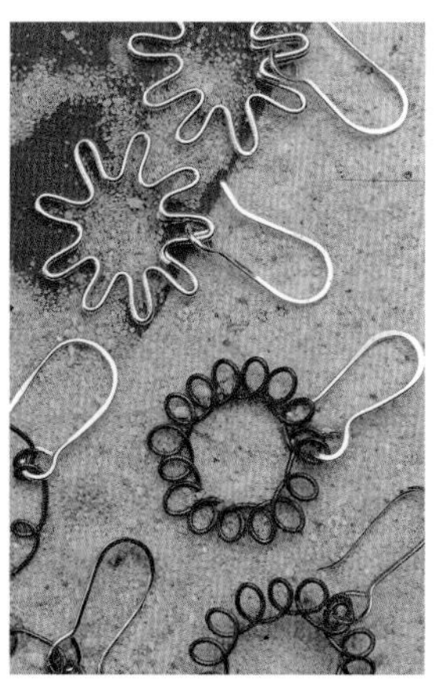

INTRODUCTION

Ellen Wieske, *Wire Vase with Stones*, 1995, steel wire and beach stones, 22 x 9 in. (55.9 x 22.9 cm), photo by artist

Years ago someone gave me a photograph from a Spanish magazine in which there were several objects made of wire. On the back of a tabletop covered with pastries was a pair of candlesticks and two pedestal baskets. I was fascinated with them. They were beautiful and so unlike anything I'd ever seen before. I found someone to translate the article for me—and was sorely disappointed to learn that the text was about the pastries and not the wonderful wire pieces!

I became obsessed with discovering where the pieces had come from, and then with learning more about this kind of work in general. I inquired in museums, antique galleries, libraries, tag sales, and thrift shops. I asked historians, collectors, junk dealers, and interior decorators. To my great satisfaction, while on my quest, I was beginning to notice wirework everywhere. Some called it seventeenth-century French pantryware; others called it Victorian; and many people said, "my grandparents had something like that."

What I learned was that many of these wire objects were made and became popular throughout Europe during the time of the Industrial Revolution. Their origins are attributed to the wireworkers in Slovakia whose work was known as *tinkering*. At first, tinkers used wire to repair other objects; for example, they wrapped wire around a broken glass bottle to keep it usable. Gradually their expertise with wire expanded, and tinkers began creating objects with wire.

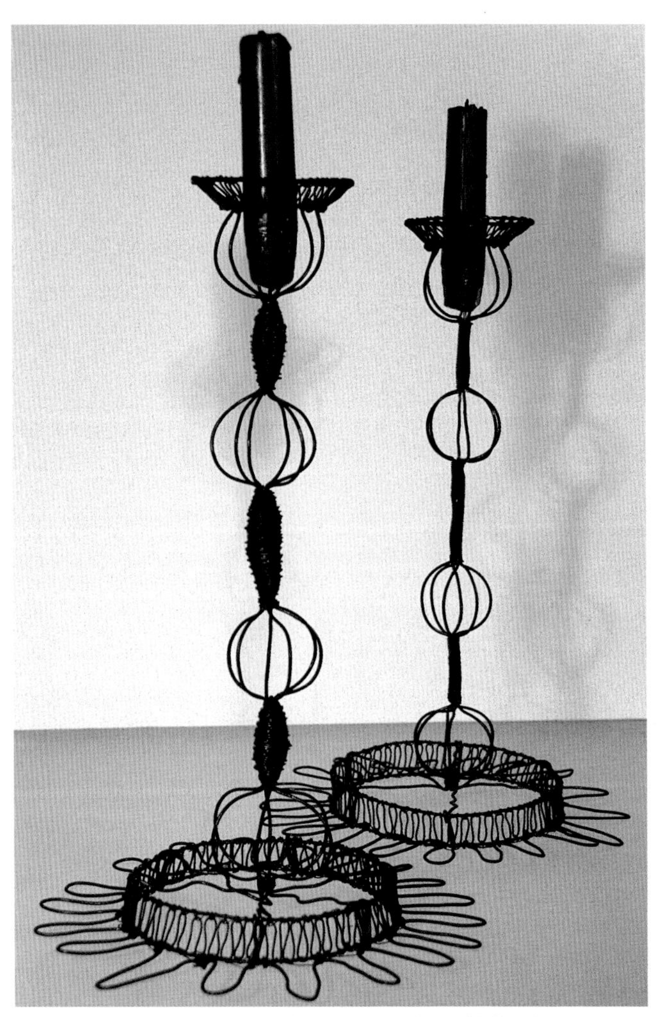

Ellen Wieske, *Candlesticks*, 1992, steel wire, 14 in. (35.6 cm), photo by artist

The tinkers and their fine skills with metal spread throughout Europe and to the United States. By 1900, when mass-produced manufactured goods were available to everyone for the first time through catalog shopping, wire products were very popular. Everyone wanted to fill their modern homes with the latest wire designs: baskets and bird-cages for the parlor; beaters, mashers, platters, griddles and dough perforators for the kitchen; planters, racks, and topiary forms for the garden; and toys and doll furniture for the children.

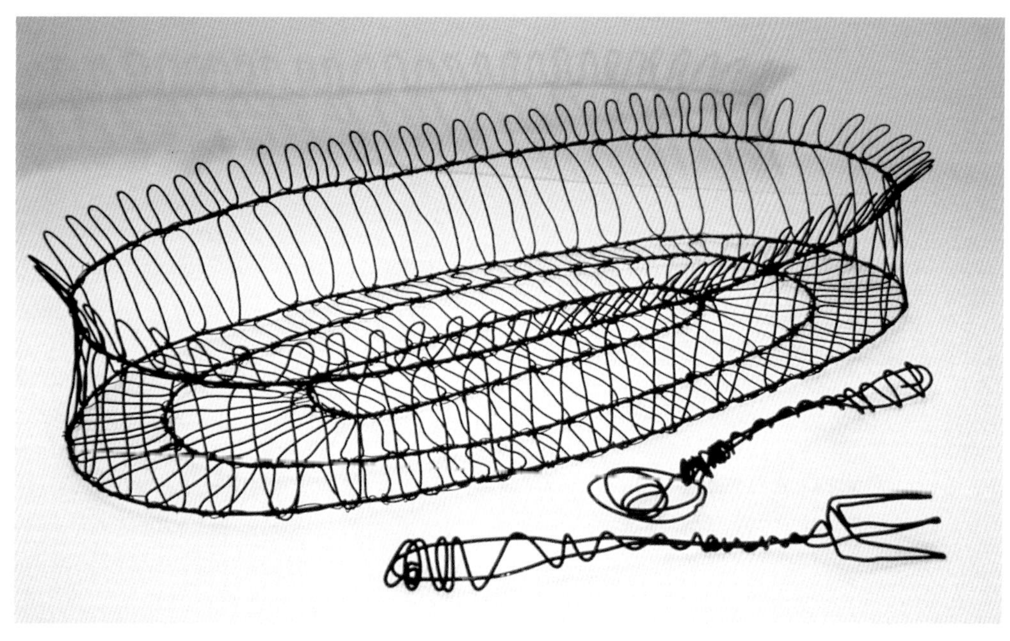

Ellen Wieske, *Basket with Utensils,* 1992, steel wire, 17 x 9 x 3 in. (43.2 x 22.9 x 7.6 cm), photo by artist

I've also been interested in wire itself—how it has been made throughout history and for what purposes it has been used. Ever since humans started making things out of metal, nearly 4,500 years ago, they have used wire. The earliest wires were made from bronze, gold, and iron, and were used to bind precious objects together or as threads to decorate special fabrics. The first known written reference to wire is in the Bible, in a description of Moses building the tabernacle and its fine decorations. "And they did beat the gold into thin plates, and cut it into wires, to work it in the blue, and in the purple, and in the scarlet, and in the fine linen, with cunning work." (Exod. 39:3)

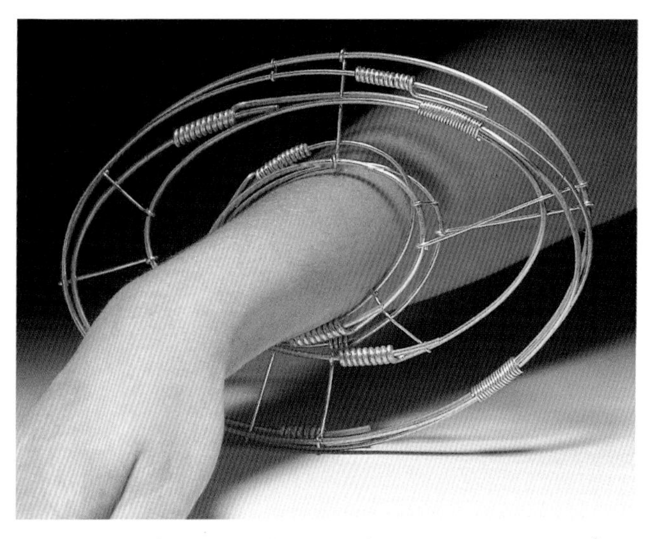

Above: Donna D'Aquino, *Wire Bracelet # 41,* sterling silver wire, 5 x 7 3/4 x 3/4 in. (12.7 x 19.7 x 1.9 cm), photo by artist

Left: Kathleen Bolan, *Abacus,* detail of pendant, sterling silver wire, Czech glass beads, and handmade lampworked glass bead with palladium leaf, photo by Tim Thayer

The chain of wire through history is fascinating. The ancient Romans held their clothing together with a device called a *fibula,* which was updated in New York in 1849 to become—the safety pin, which in turn has been keeping us together ever since! Today wire is an essential part of our lives. In one form or another, we use wire every day, from simple paper clips and staples to the electronic wiring that sends TV signals from satellites orbiting the globe.

I wanted to write this book so that I could share my enthusiasm for wire. *Wirework* will give you the ideas, the skills, and the techniques to get you started with wire.

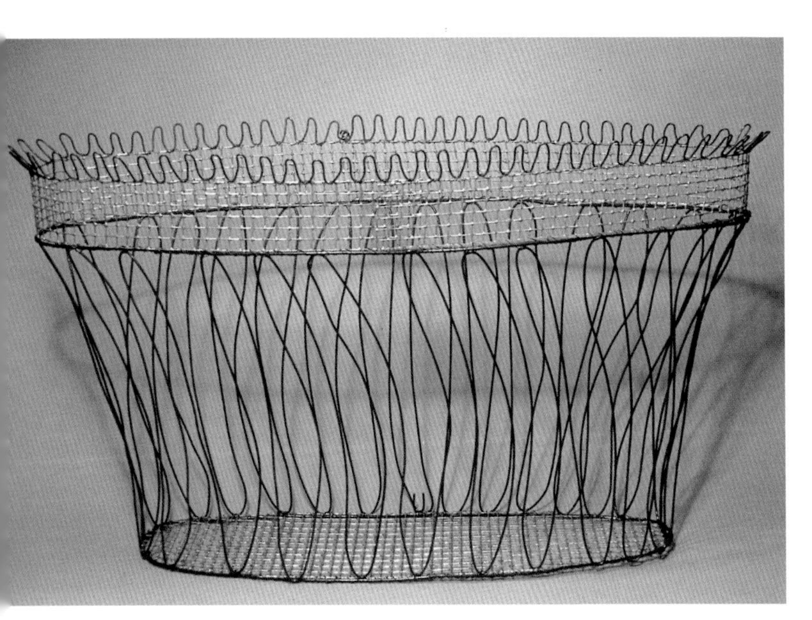

Ellen Wieske, *Basket,* 1995, steel wire, 16 x 4 x 10 in. (40.6 x 10.2 25.4 cm), photo by artist

You'll discover that wire is an enjoyable material to work with. It has a unique personality unlike any other artistic material—it's versatile, flexible, malleable, affordable, and forgiving—if you don't like what you've done with it, just cut it off or re-shape it.

No previous skill is required to learn how to work with wire. And it's wonderful how quickly you can gain a sense of accomplishment. Any of the projects can easily be made in a weekend. In fact, you can make several of the projects in one day!

Using wire is like drawing, except you get to hold and touch the "lines." Each wire object you make has the quality of a playful line drawing. It never looks like a machine made it. So even if you follow the instructions in this book to the letter, each project you make will have a unique look—one that is definitely and unmistakably all yours. That's why I love wire.

I love to teach wireworking for the same reasons. Each student has a different way of holding tools, of manipulating the wire, of joining pieces together—so when we're all working on a similar design, each of us will end up with something different.

In my workshops I've found that a lot of people love wire. From kids and adults who've never used a tool before, to fiber artists, dentists, basketmakers, and trained metalsmiths, my students have all enjoyed making things like the projects presented in this book. I hope you will enjoy the weekend in your own wire workshop!

Kristiana Tröw Spaulding, *Sandy's Room*, 2000, steel wire, 8 x 10 in. (20.3 x 25.4 cm), photo by Donald Felton, Almac Camera, San Francisco

WIREWORK BASICS

MATERIALS

To make the projects in this book, you'll need only three basic materials—wire, wire mesh, and tin cans. It's amazing how creative you can be with such simple, everyday materials, many of which are recycled, and all of which are easy to find.

Wire

Wire is metal that has been drawn into threads or long, thin rods. It's usually round in cross-section. Any metal, including gold and platinum, can be made into wire. In *Wirework* we'll work with affordable wires, such as steel, copper, brass, silver, and plastic-coated wires.

Wirework projects use many different types of affordable wires.

SOFT OR WORK-HARDENED

Wire has different states of hardness. It can be soft (*annealed*), or *work-hardened.*

Annealing is the process of heating metal, usually with a torch, to realign and relax the molecules, thereby rendering the metal soft and pliable.

Work-hardening is the opposite of annealing. It's a way to harden a piece of metal or wire by "working" it—bending, twisting, hammering, or squeezing until it becomes very stiff and unyielding.

Here's how to see work-hardening for yourself. Bend a steel paper clip back and forth. It will bend only so many times before it breaks. The molecules at the point of work suffer more and more stress until they become too hard—damage occurs and the metal snaps. This metal has been work-hardened.

This process can be altered. Bend another paper clip until it's work-hardened but not broken. Hold the hardened section over a lit match, until the metal turns red with heat. (Be sure to hold the paper clip with a vise grip or other pliers so you don't burn your fingers.) Wait for the metal to cool off. Then see how easy it is to bend again. It will remain annealed until it's once again work-hardened.

Most wire that's sold in stores has been hardened during its manufacturing process. When I'm buying wire, I try to test a small piece by bending it to see how difficult it is to bend. Some projects require a stiff wire. For others, you'll want the softest wire possible. In three projects in this book—Twisted Forks (page 24), Wired-Up Mug (page 48), and Wordy Bookmark (page 59), you'll find out how to harden wire quickly and easily.

GAUGE

Wire is measured by the thickness of its diameter, or *gauge*, according to the American Wire Gauge (AWG) standards (formerly called Brown and Sharpe [B&S] Wire Gauge). The higher the gauge number, the smaller the

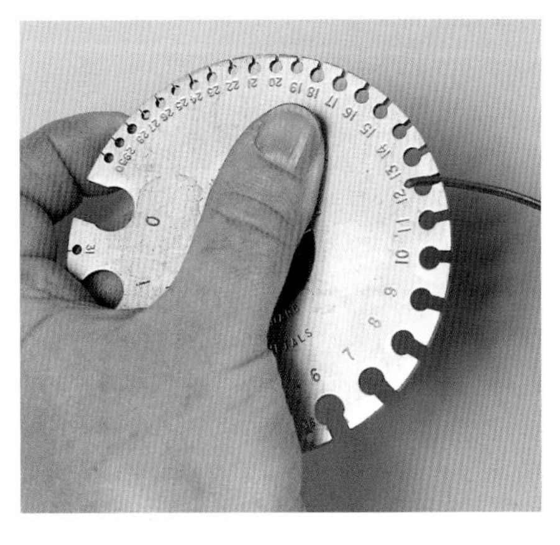

A wire gauge is a handy tool to determine the thickness, or gauge, of wire.

diameter. Thus, 30-gauge wire is as thin as a hair, whereas 6-gauge wire is as thick as a pencil. For clarity, all the wire thicknesses and project measurements in the instructions are given in both U.S. and metric versions. Just remember that conversion from U.S. to metric is not precise. Which is okay, because wireworking is not an exact science—it's artistic fun!

When shopping for wire, it's helpful to be able to recognize both types of measurements. Here's a handy conversion chart for wire gauges:

American Wire Gauge	Closest Metric Diameter in Millimeters (mm)
12	2.00 mm
14	1.50 mm
16	1.25 mm
18	1.00 mm
20	.75 mm
22	.64 mm
23	.57 mm
24	.50 mm
26	.41 mm

STEEL WIRE

Steel wire can be found in almost every hardware store, in many art and craft supply stores, and in gardening centers. There are two common types of steel wire. When the wire is a shiny silver color, or is labeled *galvanized* or *zinc-coated*, assume that it's work-hardened and therefore stiff and harder to bend. This may be exactly what you need when you're working on a large project or one that requires rigidity. Wire with a galvanized coating is best if you plan to make something that will be used outside because the coating is designed to prevent rust. Chain link fences, trash cans, and many garden tools are galvanized for this reason.

The other type of wire—annealed steel wire or *common black wire*—is my personal favorite to work with. You'll notice that most of the wire artists whose work is displayed throughout *Wirework* also like this wire. It has a dark graphite-like color, and is inexpensive and easy to find at hardware stores and art and craft suppliers. Because it's made of a low-carbon steel, it's highly susceptible to oxidation or rust. Sometimes rust is desirable, since it adds a "vintage" look. But if you don't like the effect, you can easily prevent rust from occurring by coating the steel wire with oil, paint, varnish, or wax.

Steel wire can also be treated with oil and heated in the same way that you take care of a cast iron frying pan—a good idea if the project will be used in the kitchen, or with food, such as the Twisted Forks project on page 24. Layers of olive oil that have been heated make a protective skin over the surface of the wire and prevent rust. You can do this in two different ways. Apply olive oil, then dry the wire object in an oven set on 350°F (180°C) for about 20 minutes or until it looks dry. Or spray the object with olive oil and dry it over a gas flame. Use pliers to hold it and heat it only until it begins to smoke. Let it cool, then repeat several times. The object will gradually turn blacker.

If the wire object won't come into direct contact with food, just spray it with olive oil and rub it with a cloth. Objects that won't be used in the kitchen can be sprayed with household spray wax and cleaned with a toothbrush or scrub brush.

Whenever you wash a wire piece, dry it immediately, and from time to time, spray it with olive oil and rub it. The oil will prevent air from coming in direct contact with the steel, and that's how to prevent rust. If rust does appear on something you don't want to rust, just rub it with a rough, scrubbing pad and oil it up.

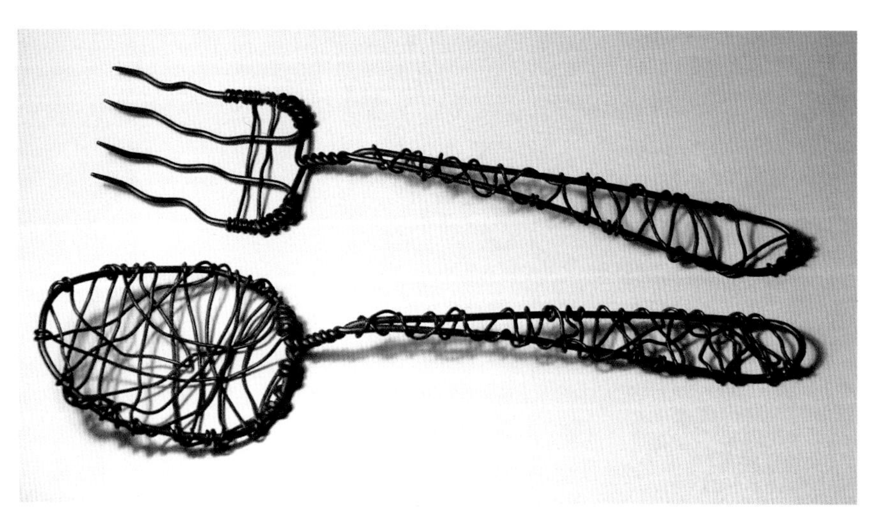

Ellen Wieske, *Salad Set,* 1995, steel wire, 13 x 3 in. (33 x 7.6 cm), photo by artist

OTHER TYPES OF WIRE

Brass and copper wire are beautiful shiny wires that give a sparkle to any project, such as the Bright and Brassy Necklace Holder on page 50. If you wish, you can also use these wires as variations of steel and color wire in many of the projects in the book. For example, I made the Bent Wire Brooch (page 26) and the Wordy Bookmark (page 59) in steel wire, but they look equally elegant in brass or copper. Both these wires can be found in hardware stores, and art and craft suppliers, and are usually sold in rolls or on spools.

Priscilla Turner Spada, *Galaxie,* 1998, necklace and earrings of handmade lampworked glass beads, sterling silver wire, 7 x 6½ x ½ in. (17.8 x 16.5 x 1.3 cm), photo by Tommy Olof Elder

Ellen Wieske, *Basket,* 1995, copper, steel and brass wire, 9 x 5 in. (22.9 x 12.7 cm), photo by artist

Aluminum wire is very easy to work with because it is so soft and pliable, as you can see from the many different shapes it takes in the Bread Lover's Bread Basket (page 55). It can be bought from art and craft suppliers.

Sterling silver wire is great for small-scale jewelry projects. It's the most expensive wire used in this book (see Looped Earrings, on page 53). It can be purchased only through jewelry suppliers and is usually sold by length.

There are two types of colored wire generally used in wirework. Both are copper but have very different looks. One type allows the copper shine to show through (such as the gleaming red wire used in Shiny Apples on page 30). These shiny wires are either chemically altered to create the color, or have had a color coating applied that will adhere permanently. They come in a wide variety of colors and are usually sold by the spool in jewelry supply and arts and crafts stores. The other

Anne Mondro, *Untitled,* 1998, copper wire necklace, 16 x 2½ x 2 in. (40.6 x 6.4 x 5.1 cm), photo by Robert Diamante

type of colored wire is plastic-coated colored wire, often called *cable* wire. It is copper wire encased in a coat of colored plastic. This wire also comes in every color in the rainbow and more, and you can find it just about anywhere—hardware stores, electronic suppliers, arts and crafts suppliers. Any time I indicate "colored wire" in a project, you can use whichever type of wire you prefer.

Advanced technologies are always being applied to wiremaking, so keep your eyes open in the arts and crafts supply shops for the newest wires to hit the market.

Ellen Wieske, *Bread Knives,* 1997, steel wire, tin, nickel, 14 x $1^1/_2$ in. (35.6 x 3.8 cm), photo by artist

DETERMINING HOW MUCH WIRE YOU'LL NEED

Here's a quick and easy way to figure out how much wire you may need for a project. Sketch the project on a piece of paper first. Next, bend some very thin wire along the lines you sketched, as if you were tracing them with the wire. Then straighten out the wire and measure it. Always add a few inches to give yourself some leeway.

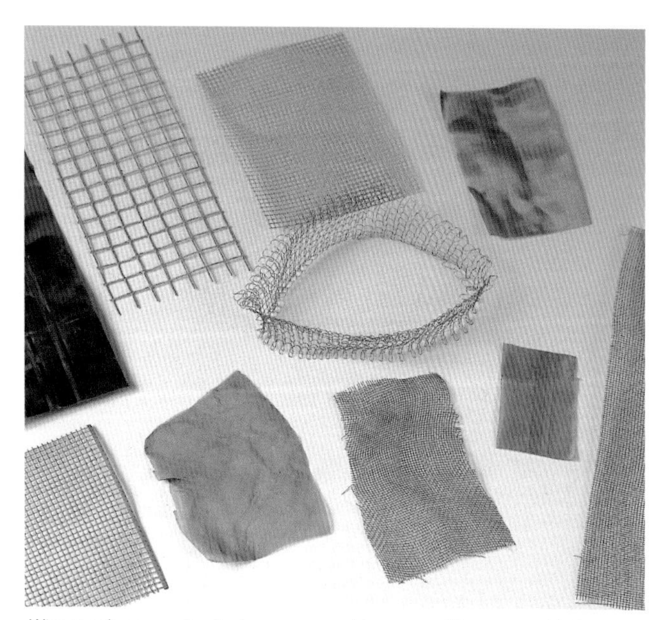
Wire mesh comes in steel, copper, and brass—and in many grid sizes.

As a general rule when deciding how much wire you need, it's better to have a little too much than not enough. Besides, you can always make wonderful projects with pieces of leftover wire, such as the Fancy-Free Flower Hooks (page 35) and the Handy Catch-All Basket (page 39).

Wire Mesh

Many types of screens, or *mesh*, are made of wire and are excellent materials to play with. A thick, large-grid steel screen known as *carpenters cloth* or *hardware cloth* is used in the See-Through Mesh Box project (page 37). Screens are made in copper and brass, too. Mesh material can be found in hardware stores and industrial suppliers.

Tin

Tin cans with printed designs work wonderfully with wire. I've used them in two projects, Tin Star Ornaments (page 28) and Sassy Salad Set (page 63). Tin cans are easy to work with once you've cut them open and flattened them out. You can find pretty tins in the grocery store, especially among imported products such as olive oil, tomato sauce, loose tea, candy, and cookies.

TOOLS

You need very few specialized tools to make the projects in this book. Check around your house for hammers, pliers, cutters, nails, marking tools, and scrap wood. Chances are good that you will find what you need to get started without leaving home.

If you do find that you want to get a few tools, check first at your local hardware store. Keep your eyes open for tools (and wire and other supplies, too) at art or craft suppliers, sewing stores, flower-arranging shops, tag sales, jewelry suppliers, flea markets, used tool or salvage yards, or on the Internet.

Pliers

Pliers are tools with a pair of pivoting jaws, used for bending, cutting, and holding things. Pliers come in a variety of configurations. Some are used for general purposes and others have very specific functions. Following are the pliers you may already have—or will want to get—beginning with the most common and general-purpose types.

Wire cutters are pliers that cut wire. They vary in style and price. Good wire cutters are a worthy investment. They don't have to be expensive or new, but they shouldn't be rusted, and their cutting edges should be smooth. To test a pair of wire cutters, press the jaws together and hold them up to the light—if no light can be seen through the area where the cutting edges meet, then they'll deliver a complete cut.

Common, or *slip-joint pliers* can be found in any basic tool set. They're a great tool to start with and are very useful to have in your collection. They usually have a serrated or heavily textured surface on the inside pincer, or *jaw*. The jaws can be adjusted into two different sizes by sliding the one jaw forwards or back at the intersection.

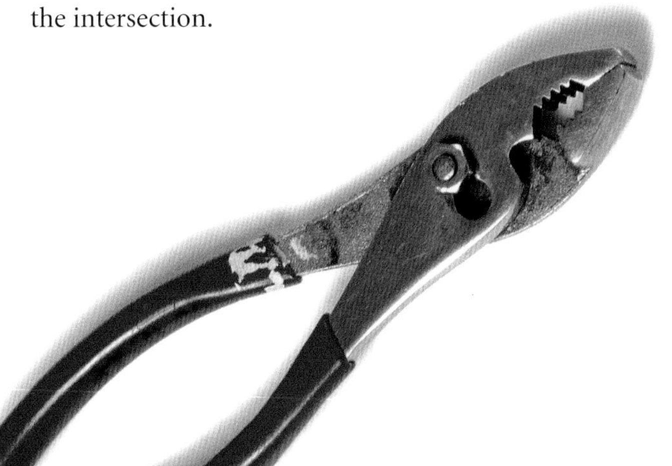

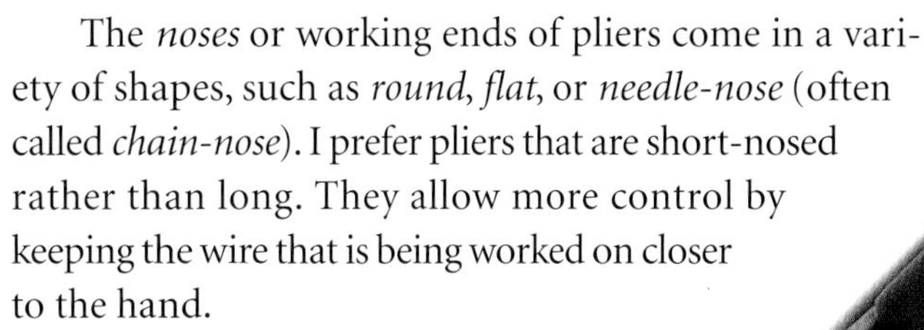

The *noses* or working ends of pliers come in a variety of shapes, such as *round*, *flat*, or *needle-nose* (often called *chain-nose*). I prefer pliers that are short-nosed rather than long. They allow more control by keeping the wire that is being worked on closer to the hand.

The jaws can be textured or smooth. Textured jaws give more gripping power but will mar the wire surface, especially on soft metals, such as copper and silver. Smooth jaws leave the metal unharmed but they may slip. Wrap masking tape around the nose of any pliers to prevent scratching the wire or to give smooth jaws more grip.

Parallel pliers offer a unique advantage. Their jaws move parallel to each other rather than away from a single pivot point, providing a strong, solid grip that runs the length of the jaws. Parallel pliers can be difficult to find and expensive. Jewelry tool suppliers have them, as well as sporting goods stores with fishing departments. Parallel pliers come in needle-nose, and flat-nose styles, as well as textured and smooth jaws. Slip-joint pliers adjusted to their large jaw setting can be used as an alternative to parallel pliers.

Vise grip pliers come in a variety of sizes, nose shapes, and jaw textures. I like the small, flat-nose styles. These are terrific because they have a mechanism that allows the pliers to remain closed without your having to squeeze the handles, leaving your hands free. I use these often for twisting or filing.

Patterning Tools—Jigs

Patterns are one of the distinctive characteristics of wirework projects. Repeated patterns, what I call *yardage* or *ribbons*, add visual weight, order, rhythm, or balance to your projects, filling in areas of what would otherwise look like skimpy "line drawings." Many of the projects in this book require patterns. To make them, you'll need to make and use a wonderful tool called a *jig*.

A jig is any device that allows you to create and repeat accurately a shape or pattern. Instead of relying on your hands and eyes to make a pattern over and over again, you just bend the wire back and forth around the nails on a jig. Two types of jigs are used for the projects in this book: simple flat jigs made of wood, and round wooden dowels.

FLAT WOODEN JIGS–FIXED AND ADJUSTABLE

There are two types of flat wooden jigs. The easiest to make is the "fixed" jig—unless you remove the nails in this jig, it's permanent, or "fixed." The adjustable jig is more versatile because you can easily "adjust" the configuration of the nails to make different patterns. You can make both jigs from any flat piece of wood, including a scrap of wood. Hardwoods (such as maple, oak, or ash) are best because they hold up better, but I have made jigs out of pine, too, and they work very well

The tools for patterning wire are easy to make and use.

MAKING A FIXED JIG

Each fixed jig has just one configuration, meaning it's the easiest jig to make. In my workshop, I use many fixed jigs with different configurations.

YOU WILL NEED
Piece of flat wood
Small nails or brads
Hammer
Ruler
Pencil

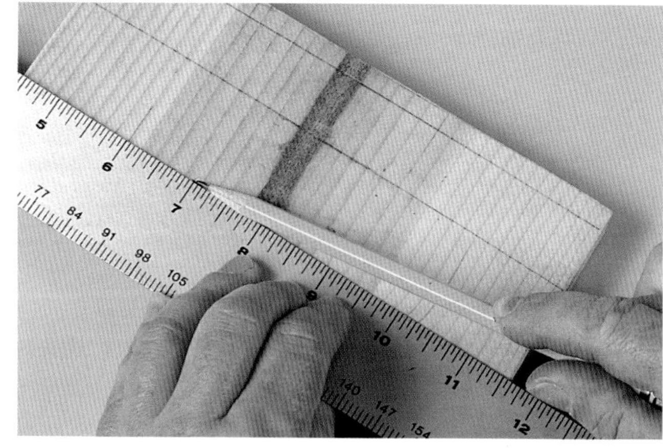

1 With the pencil and ruler, draw a grid on the piece of wood. First draw parallel lines down the length of the wood.

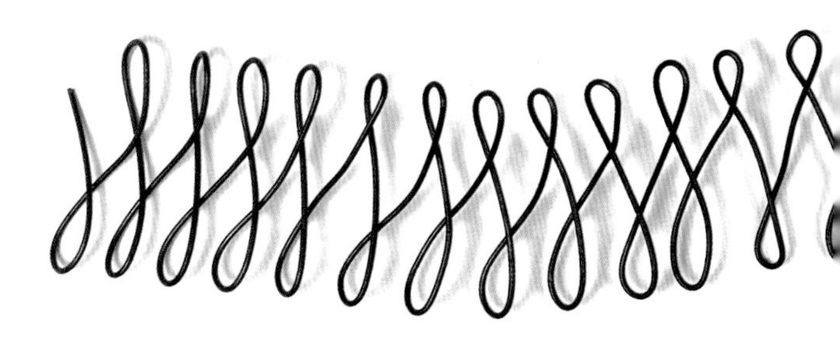

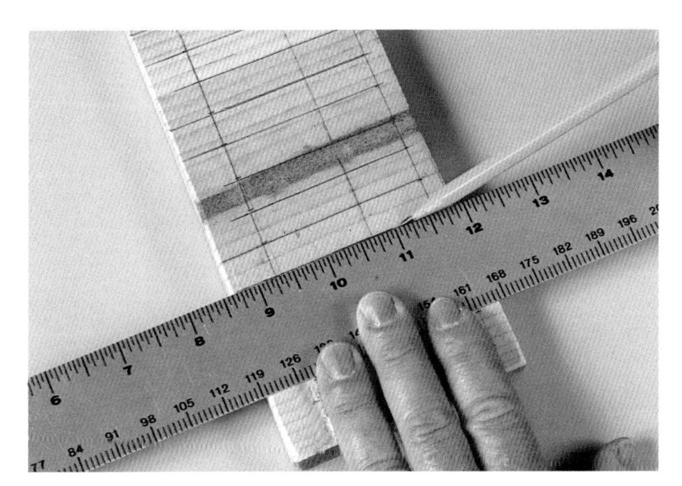

2 Then draw intersecting parallel lines across the width of the wood.

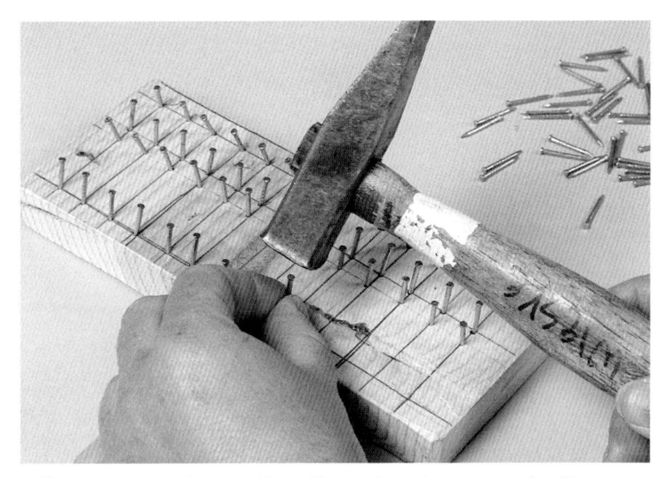

3 Hammer in small nails or brads where the lines intersect. The sample shown here is in 1/2-inch (1.3 cm) increments. You can create a pattern in any shape by arranging the nails in any configuration.

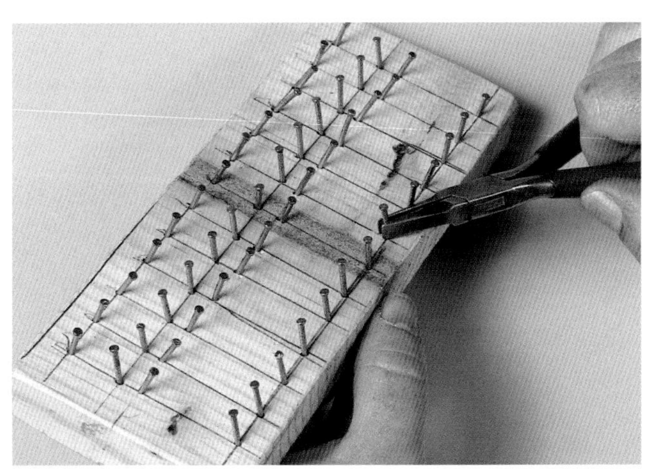

4 Be sure to angle the nails slightly towards the center of the rows, so the wire will slip off them easily after bending.

MAKING AN ADJUSTABLE JIG

With the adjustable jig, you can move the nails around in it, thus allowing you to change patterns easily. It requires more time and tools to make than the fixed jig, but the fun you have using it is well worth the effort.

YOU WILL NEED
Piece of flat wood
Drill, hand-operated or electric
#35 drill bit, 7/64 inches (11.1 mm)
2-inch (5.1 cm) 6d common nails
Hammer
Bolt cutter
Ruler
Pencil

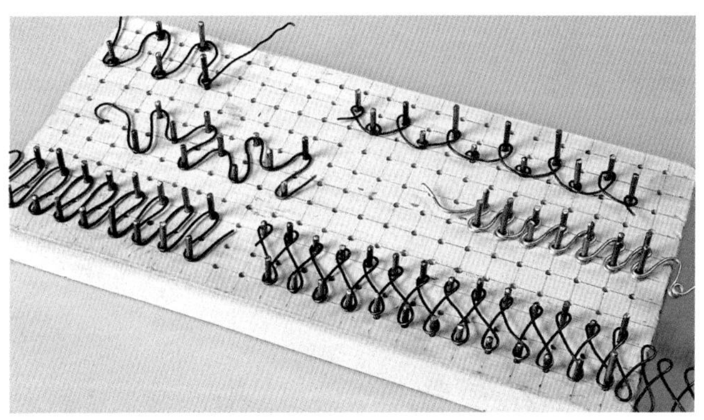

1 With the pencil and ruler, draw a 1/2-inch (1.3 cm) grid onto the piece of wood.

2 Drill holes all the same depth at the intersections of the marked lines. This can be done by using a drill press with the height gauge set or by using tape to mark the depth on the drill bit. Nails will slip in and out of the drilled holes.

3 Clip off the nail ends with the bolt cutters. If you leave the heads on, it will be more difficult to remove the patterned wire.

ROUND DOWEL JIGS

By wrapping wire around a dowel, you can create coils, which can be used to make many interesting patterns. For simplicity, in our projects we used only two different sizes of wooden dowels, but any long metal or wooden rod can be used as a dowel in wirework.

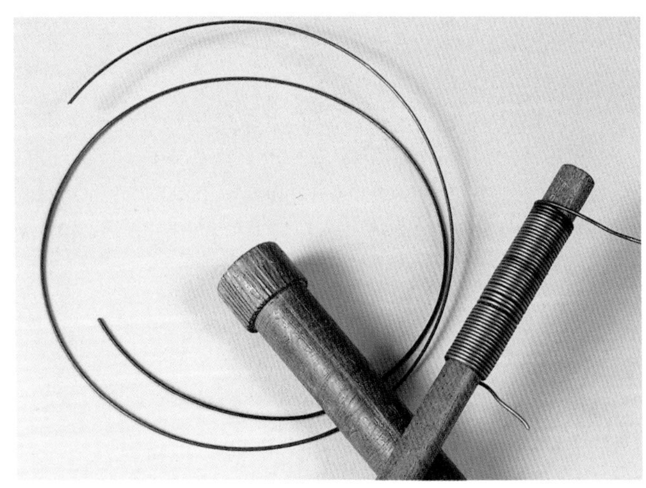

It's easy to wrap wire around wooden dowels to create coils and springs.

Hammering Tools and Surfaces

Hammers come in lots of shapes and can be made from different materials. Their shapes vary widely, from claws to all sorts of peens. The *peen* end or *face* can be round, oval, square, or rectangular, and can be flat, slightly domed, or ball shaped.

Steel hammers are the most common hammers. Most steel hammerheads are centered on a wooden handle and have two different ends. For example, the hammer that most of us are familiar with is the steel claw hammer. It has two claws on one end for removing nails, and a round flat face on the other end for pounding nails into wood.

Hammerheads are also made out of *rawhide, rubber, plastic, brass,* and *wood.* Hammers made from these materials are very useful for working with wire or other metals because they're softer than what they're striking. Steel hammers will crush the metal—but soft hammers won't. They'll smooth or straighten the metal, but they won't mar its surface. A plastic hammer with sand inside the head, called a *sand hammer* or *dead blow,* is excellent for the wireworker. When you use this hammer it doesn't bounce. Instead, it delivers a "dead blow." It's my favorite hammer.

When you hammer a piece of wire, it's important to choose the proper surface to hammer against. A soft surface, such as a flat wooden board or a wooden tabletop, is a good choice for simple shaping or smoothing of metal shapes.

An *anvil* is a great tool for wireworking. It can be used with any soft or steel hammer for shaping wire, and is very useful for removing kinks, and for flattening, pressing, or texturing wire. Many bench vises have anvil shapes or flat places on them that can be used for these purposes. If you don't have an anvil, use a smooth piece of steel.

Shaping Tools

A *mandrel*, or a metal rod or bar, often tapered, is used as a base to shape and bend wire. Almost anything you have around the house can be used as a mandrel—a piece of pipe or tube, or a broken-off metal chair leg.

A straining cone helps shape rings.

A wooden dimensional shape, such as a *straining cone* or a baseball bat, works great for shaping rings. A hardwood (maple, for example) is always best to use. Softwoods, such as pine, aren't firm enough; the wire will just sink into them. When shaping wire with a wooden shape, use a soft hammer, such as a rawhide hammer.

Holding Tools

It's handy to have tools that hold onto things when both your hands are required elsewhere. The most important holding tool is the vise. It can be any size, and in any condition. C-clamps are useful for holding wires and tools, and all sorts of things together. For lighter holding jobs, masking tape works just fine.

A bench pin—a small piece of wood with a slot cut into it—allows me to get my hands around the object I'm working on and keeps the table surface from getting scratched. I use a C-clamp to clamp a bench pin to the edge of my worktable. Bench pins are common tools used by bench jewelers and can be purchased from a jewelry supply store.

Finishing Tools

Finishing work is the cleaning up that you may need to do to the rough ends of wires. Not much finishing will be required on the projects in this book, but when it is necessary, you'll need a few special tools.

Most home workshops have the simple holding and finishing tools for wirework.

FILES

Files come in different sizes, shapes, and textures. The surface texture is called the *tooth* or *cut* of the file. Files are numbered to indicate their texture, from coarse to smooth. Cut #00 is the coarsest and #8 is the smoothest. I suggest two files for your toolbox—a medium/coarse one, and a fine one. A coarse file works quickly and leaves a rough surface; a smooth file does finer work. The shape of the file is not very important when you're working with wire. A file with a flat surface will be perfect.

While filing, remember that the teeth of a file work on the push stroke. As you *push* the file away from your body, the file does its work best.

SANDPAPER

Sandpaper is similar to a file, but instead of referring to its coarseness as its tooth or cut, we refer to sandpaper's *grit*. Grit is an indication of the number of bits of sand per square inch. The higher the grit number, the smoother the sandpaper. You'll need a coarse piece, like #220, and a fine piece, like #400. I like to wrap a piece of sandpaper around a square stick and use it like a file. While a file cuts only on the push stroke, however, the sandpaper works in any direction. Always start a finishing job with coarse sandpaper and end it with smooth.

Emery boards and nail files are also wonderful tools for filing and sanding wires. Scouring pads or steel wool are very useful to shine or even out a finish. They also remove rust very nicely.

Measuring and Marking Tools

A tape measure, a ruler, and marking tools such as chalk, wax pencils, china markers, or felt-tip markers will be easy to find around the house.

Tin-Working Tools

Tools for tin are basically those that will cut it. You'll need a can opener to cut off the tops and bottoms, and snips to cut through the thick seam. You can use regular household scissors—not your best pair—to cut out shapes from the opened tin. Always use gloves when cutting tin.

Safety Tools

Keep gloves and safety protective glasses on hand, and bandages nearby, just in case.

TECHNIQUES

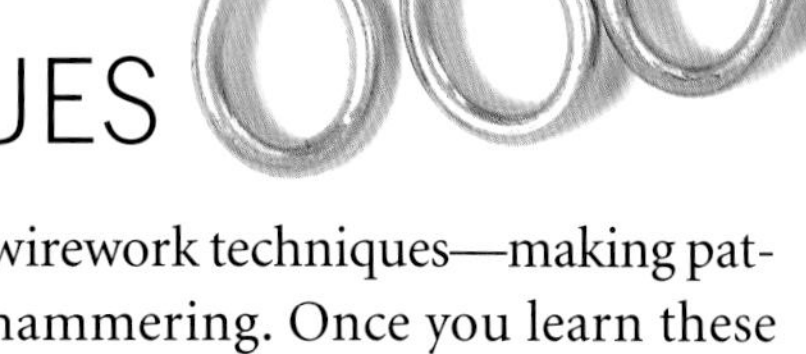

There are three basic wirework techniques—making patterns, twisting, and hammering. Once you learn these basics, you can create nearly limitless variations on the original design of any wire project.

Patterning Techniques

There are seven projects in this book that use patterns. Take a look at them now to see the wide range of possibilities: Garden Candleholder (page 41), Round Trivet (page 44), Wild Flowers (page 46), Bright and Brassy Necklace Holder (page 50), Looped Earrings (page 53), Bread Lover's Bread Basket (page 55), and Interlocking Letter Rack (page 61).

MAKING PATTERNS ON THE FLAT WOODEN JIGS

Using a jig is the easiest way to make patterns. Just bend the wire back and forth around the nails. The farther apart the nails in your configuration are, the longer or wider the bends in your pattern will be.

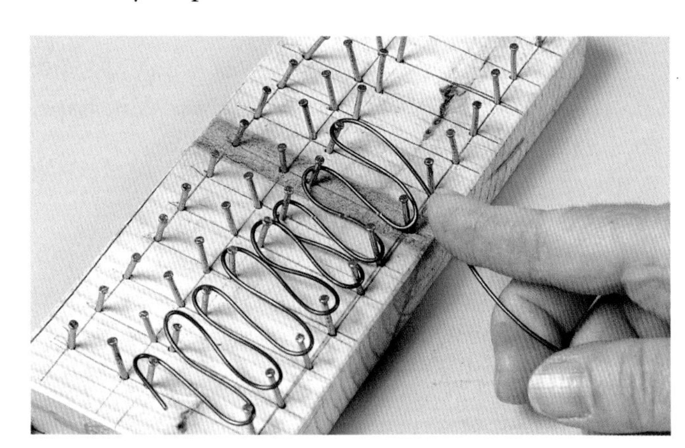

MAKING PATTERNS ON THE ROUND WOODEN DOWELS

Making patterns on the dowel requires two basic steps: wrapping the wire on the dowel and shaping it afterwards.

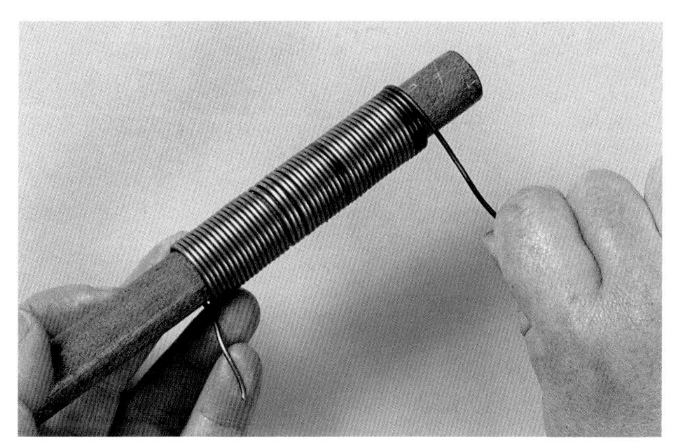

1 When you wrap the wire, keep 3 to 4 inches (7.6 to 10.2 cm) free at the beginning, and hold onto it to keep the coil from sliding around on the dowel.

2 To rearrange the coils made on the dowels into different ribbons of pattern, you can flatten, spread, and stretch them out. You can use either the anvil or the tabletop as your hammering surface. Start by using a sand hammer or rawhide hammer to slowly and gently push over the top edge of the coil.

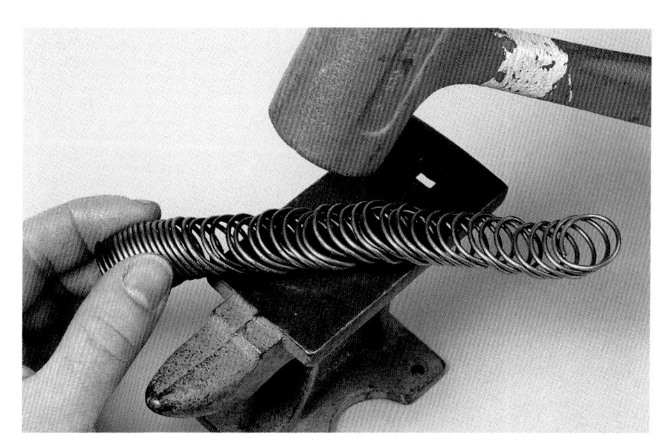

3 Continue hammering lightly at an angle, working the coil until it's flattened out.

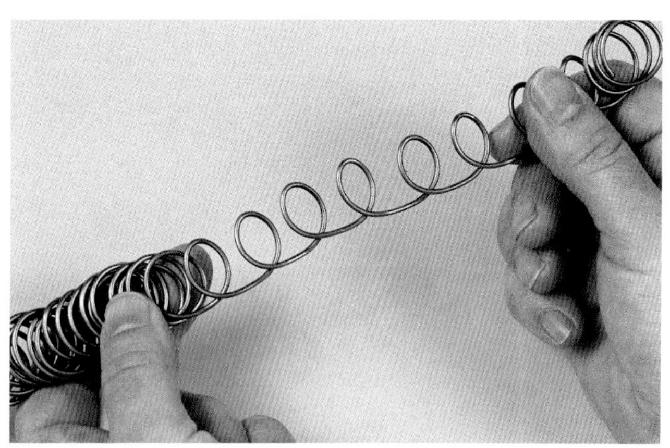

4 With your fingers, gradually spread out the flattened coils, a little bit at a time. Once you have them spread out, re-flatten the coils with the hammer. Spread, flatten, and stretch until you find the pattern you like.

ATTACHING PATTERNED PIECES

When you attach a patterned piece to another piece of wire, you're simply wrapping the pieces together with wire instead of thread. To make a nice seamless look, overlap the two ends of the pattern slightly, and wrap them securely with the stitching wire. Cut off any loose ends.

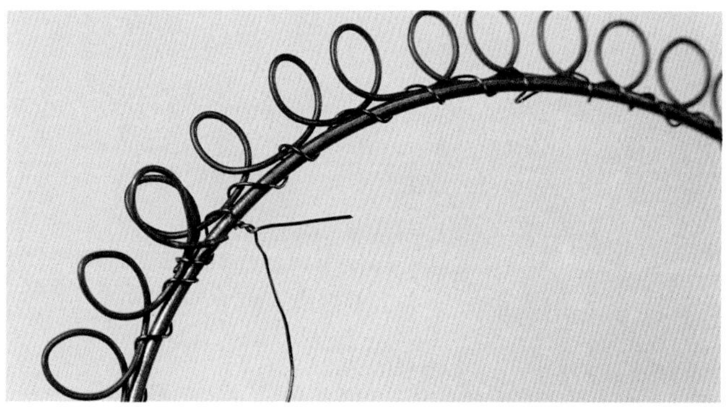

Kathleen Bolan, Black Light, 1999, sterling silver wire bracelet, $7^{1}/_{2}$ in. (19.1 cm) with handmade lampworked dichroic glass beads, photo by Tim Thayer

Christine Clark, *Befitting of the Circumstances*, 2000, steel wire, encaustic paints over wood, 4 x 30 x 7 in. (10.2 x 76.2 x 17.8 cm), photo by Bill Bachhuber

USING PLIERS AS A JIG

You can use your flat-nose pliers as a jig when you need a tiny pattern. The shape of the pliers will determine the pattern.

Move the nose of the pliers up the length of the wire, bending it back and forth to create the pattern.

Above: Christine Clark, *Hair Receivers I and II*, 1998, steel wire, human hair, 20 x 5 x 4 in. (50.8 x 12.7 x 10.2 cm) and 19 x 6 x 4.5 in. (48.3 x 15.2 x 11.4 cm), photo by Bill Bachhuber

Left: Ellen Wieske, *Wire Cup Drawing*, 1991, steel wire, approx. 3 x 5 in. (7.6 x 12.7 cm), photo by artist

MAKING SPIRALS

Spirals are a favorite pattern in wirework, and artists love to incorporate them in their designs. See the Hanging Photo Holder (page 32) and the Interlocking Letter Rack (page 61).

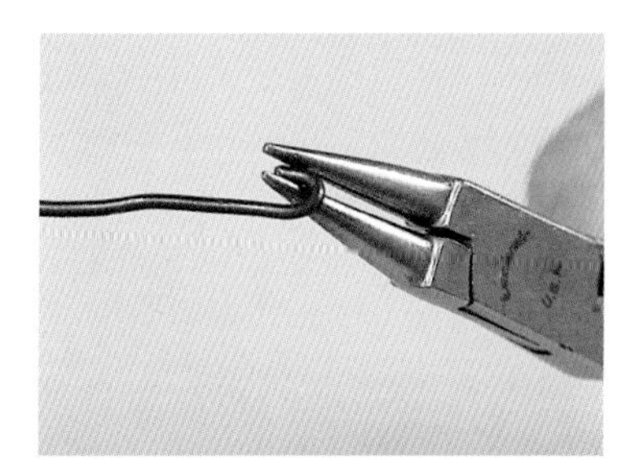

1 Use round-nose pliers to start bending the wire into a spiral.

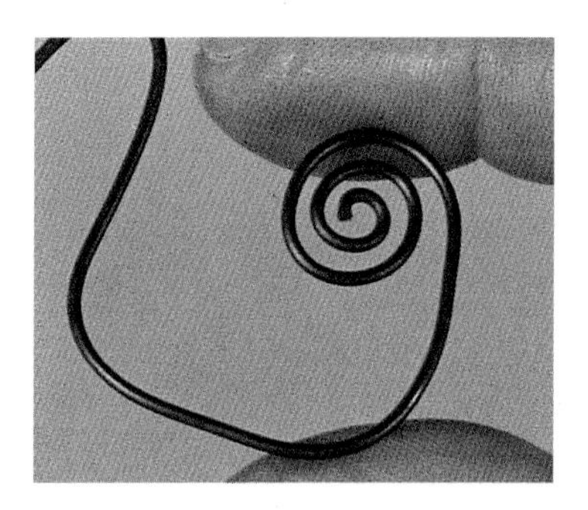

2 As you continue the curl farther along, use flat-nose pliers, or your fingers.

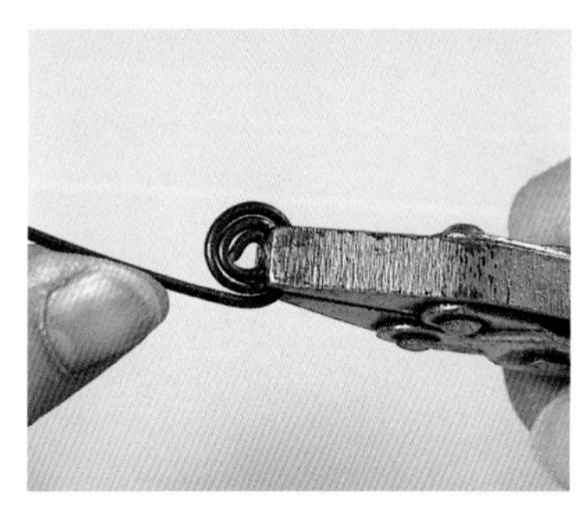

3 Depending on the type and size of the curl you're making, you might want to use parallel-jaw pliers or slip-joint pliers to finish it.

Twisting

Twisting wires together work-hardens them and results in a thicker, stronger wire, such as you'll need for the Fancy-Free Flower Hooks (page 35), and enables you to make large-scale wire projects. Twisted wire also gives variety to your designs, such as the handles for the Twisted Forks (page 24).

Any two wires can be twisted together. Although the resulting wire is thicker, it's not that much harder to bend than a single wire. So if you want to make something that requires a large-gauge wire, and you don't have enough on hand, you don't have to go out and buy thick wire, just twist two thinner wires together.

TWISTING A WIRE

YOU WILL NEED

Wire

Vise

Vise grip pliers

Drill, hand-operated or electric

Small cup hook from the hardware store

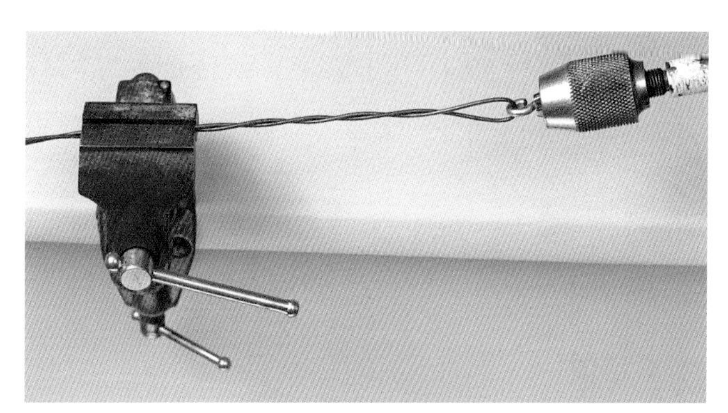

1 Bend the wire (or wires) in half to make a loop. Clamp into the vise all the loose ends of the wires. Slip the wire loop onto the small cup hook. Insert the hook into the chuck of the drill. (If you don't have a drill, clamp the ends with vise grip pliers.)

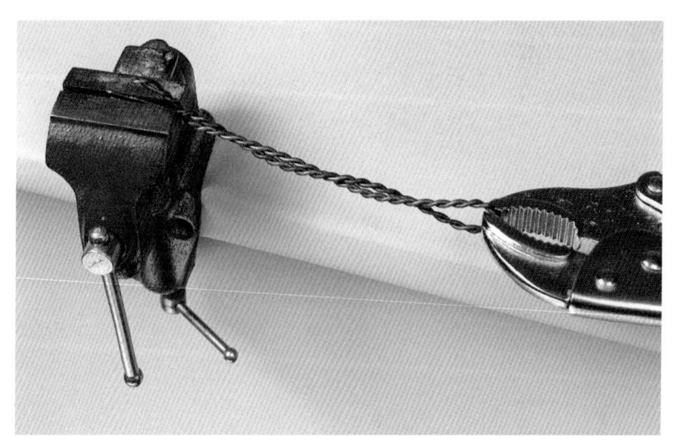

2 Pull back on the wires until there is no slack, then twist them with the drill or pliers.

3 Keep twisting until you have the thickness or style you want. If you have difficulty twisting the wires with the drill, clamp them with the vise grip pliers and twist them by hand.

For a peppermint-stripe look, twist two different colored wires together. Try four different colors for a more colorful pattern.

For a 4-strand twist, bend one piece of wire in half, clamp the two loose ends in the vise, and twist the wire by hand or with the drill. Now bend this twisted wire in half, clamp the loose ends in the vise, and twist again.

For a really cool, complex pattern, try this technique: First completely twist two wires to the right. Then, completely twist a second pair of wires to the left. Place both twisted pairs together and twist all four in one direction, either to the right or to the left.

For an unusual textured look, twist two different gauges of wire together, such as 26-gauge (.41 mm) and 16-gauge (1.25 mm).

Hammering Techniques

Hammering is used in wirework to create a final, finished look on individual wires, especially when they're highly visible, such as in jewelry, and projects like Wordy Bookmark (page 59) and the fork tines in Twisted Forks (page 24). The hammering tool you use determines what kind of mark will result. For example, in the photo below, the marks on the wire on the left were made with the flat end of the hammerhead; the ones on the right were made with the sharp end. The condition of the hammer face also determines the look of the mark. A smooth, polished face will make a shiny dimple or mark. A hammer face that is rusted or damaged will make marks that look chewed up and rough.

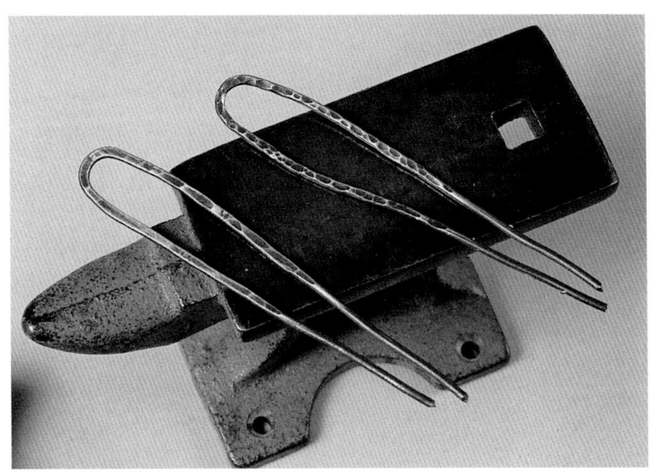

A flat hammerhead made the marks on the wire on the left. A sharp hammerhead made the marks on the right.

Practice hammering on a scrap of wire or metal to see what the hammer marks will look like before you hit your real work. When hammering, never smash wires that cross over each other. They will bite into each other and break at the point where they cross.

Ellen Wieske, *Flatware*, 1995, steel wire, approx. 7 in. each (17.8 cm), photo by artist

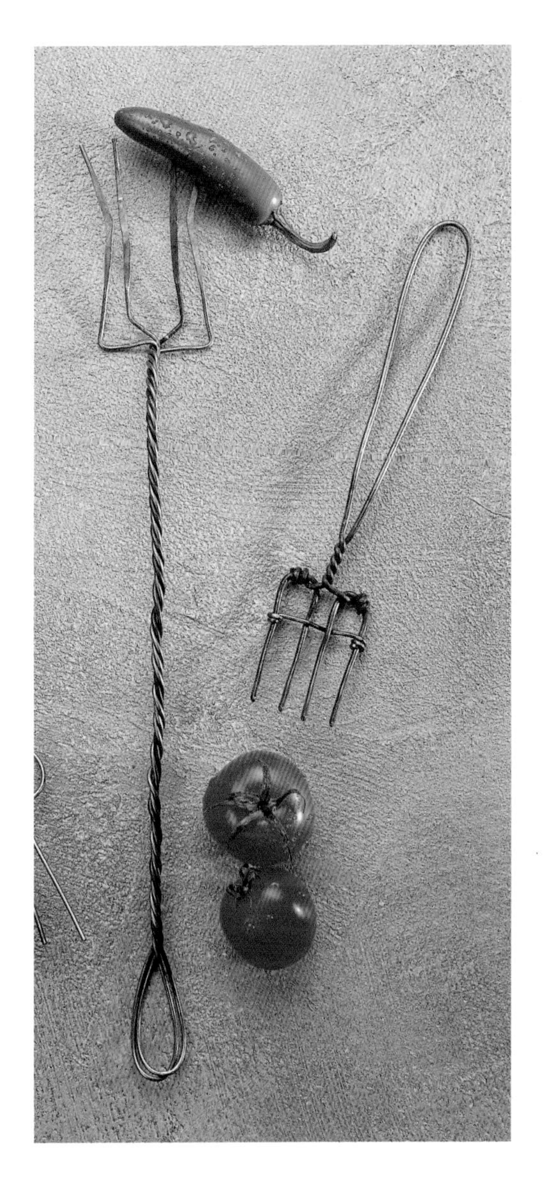

WIREWORK PROJECTS

I selected a variety of projects for this book, some easy, others more challenging. It is my hope that as you work through the projects, you'll find your abilities and understanding of tools and materials will improve. May you enjoy the journey and the results of your efforts. And may you have lots of fun along the way.

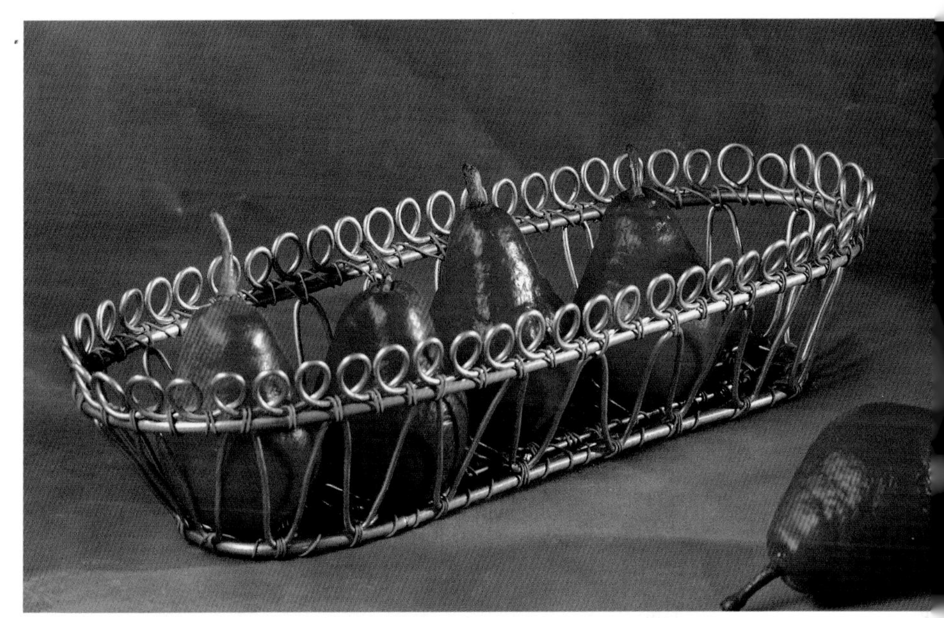

Twisted Forks

Hung on a wall or used at a barbecue, these elegant wire forks add a touch of class to any setting. They're great fun to make, too—you just twist, cut, and shape.

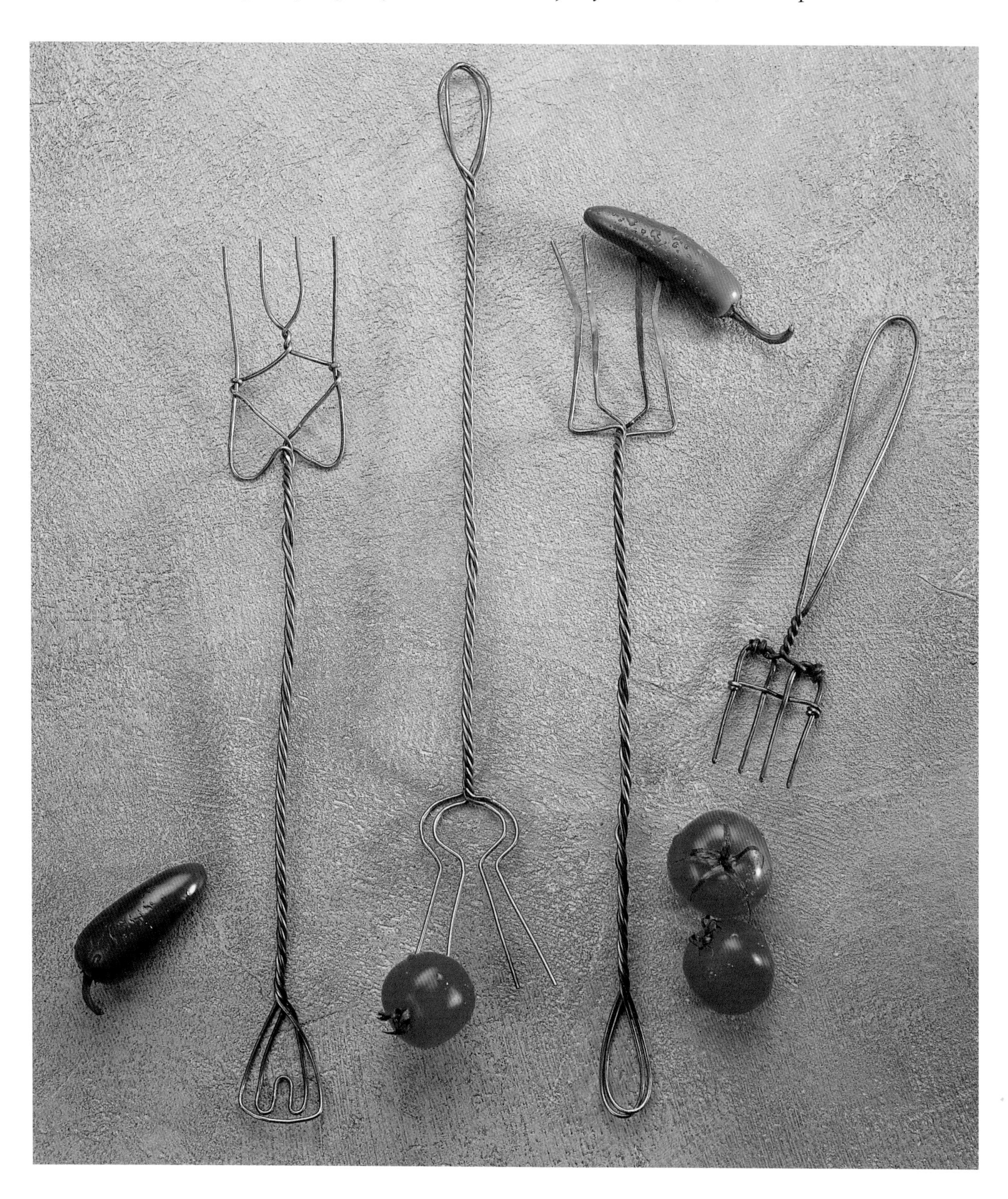

YOU WILL NEED

14-gauge (1.50 mm) steel or brass wire, 52 inches (1.32 m) in length

Wire cutters

Vise

Vise grip pliers

Flat-nose pliers

Sand hammer

Steel hammer

Anvil or smooth piece of steel (optional)

BEFORE YOU START

Re-read the sections on twisting (page 21) and on hammering (page 22) in the Wirework Basics.

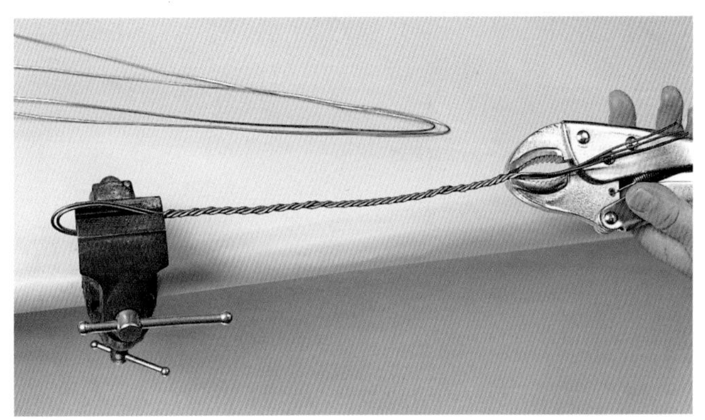

1 Cut the wire in half. Bend in half each of the two resulting 26-inch (66 cm) pieces of wire to make a loop at their ends. Put 2 inches (5.1 cm) of both loops into the vise. As shown in the photo, use the vise grip pliers, twist 9 inches (22.9 cm) of the wires together, leaving 4 inches (10.2 cm) free at the ends.

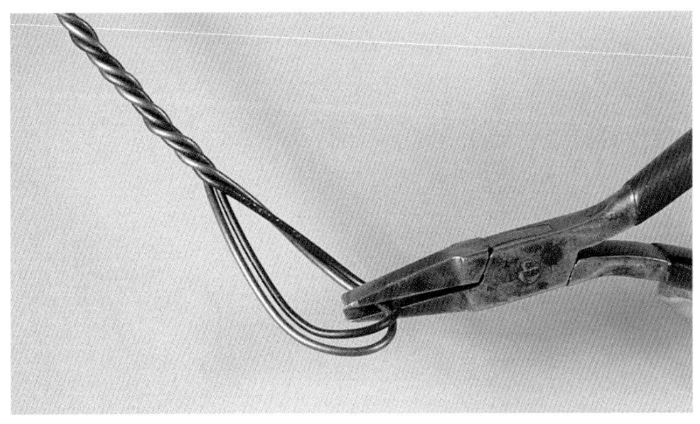

2 With your fingers or the flat-nose pliers, shape the looped ends of the twisted wires to make the handles.

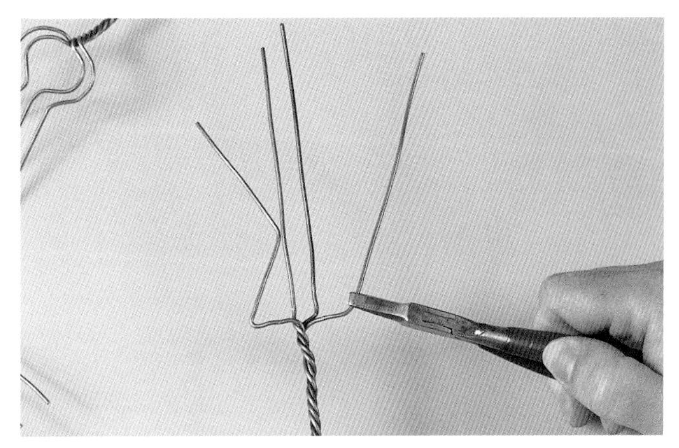

3 With your fingers or the flat-nose pliers, shape the four 4-inch (10.2 cm) wires on their loose end to make the fork tines.

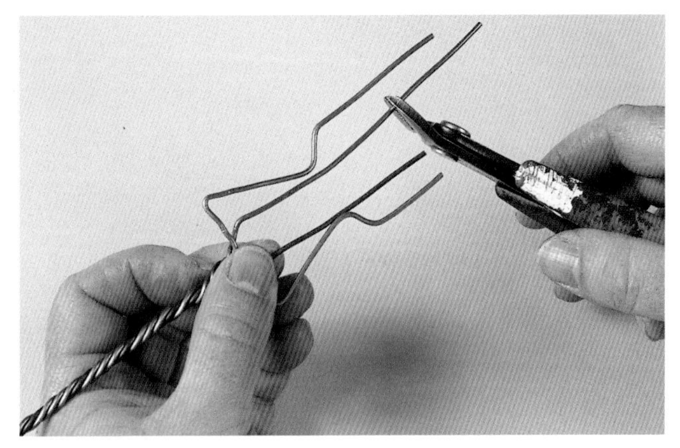

4 Flatten both ends with the sand hammer. Trim the ends with wire cutters to make the tines even in length.

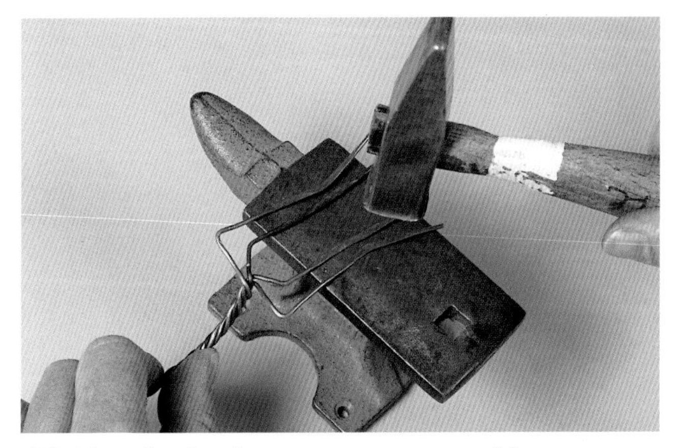

5 To make the tines stronger, use a steel hammer to flatten them against an anvil or smooth piece of steel. Remember, never crush crossed wires.

Bent Wire Brooch

It's fun and easy to create wearable art with this simple brooch project. All you do is take a length of wire, bend it into any shape you want, and follow a few basic rules for the mechanics of pin workings. Start with a sketch—or just go at it! Either way, you'll make a unique fashion statement.

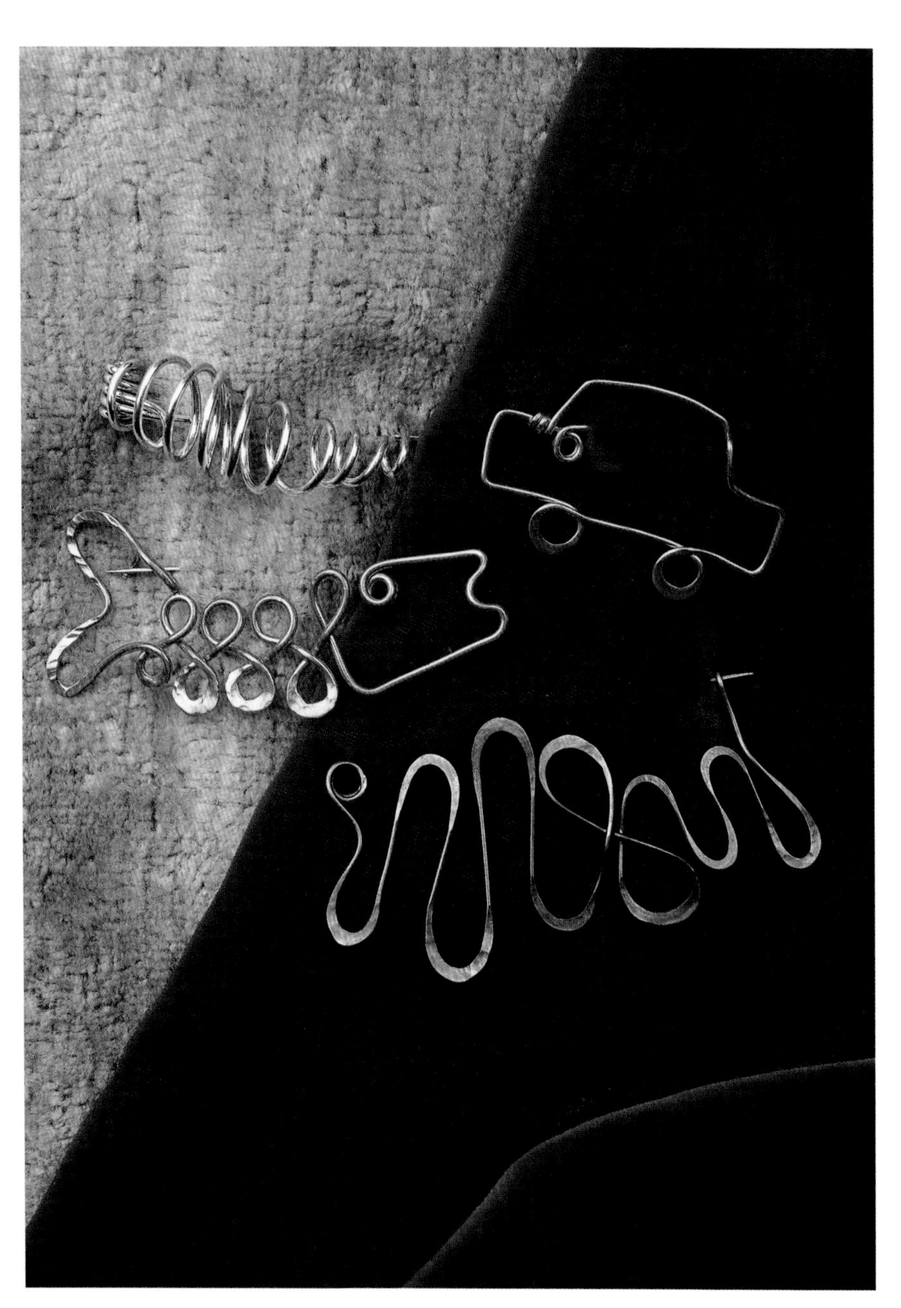

YOU WILL NEED

- 14- or 16-gauge (1.50 mm or 1.25 mm) wire, 20 inches (50.8 cm) in length, depending on your design
- Vise
- Vise grip pliers
- Round-nose pliers
- Flat-nose pliers
- Wire cutters
- File
- Sandpaper or emery board

BEFORE YOU START

The pin stem of a brooch gets a lot of use as it is pushed through fabric, so it needs to be strengthened. See the section on work-hardening in Wirework Basics on page 9.

For a colorful variation, wrap colored wire around the brooch pattern.

1 To make the pin stem: Hold one end of the wire in the vise, leaving 4 inches (10.2 cm) sticking out. Use the vise grip pliers to twist the 4-inch (10.2 cm) end until it breaks off at the vise grip end. The end that remains on the length of the wire is the pin stem and is now work-hardened.

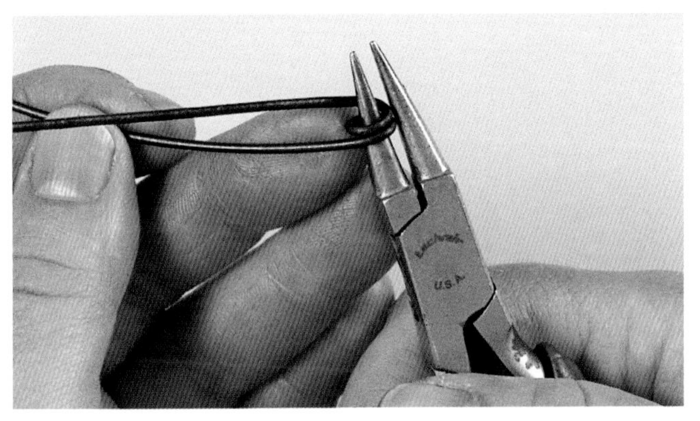

2 To make the pin spring: Position the round-nose pliers about 2 inches (5.1 cm) from the end of the wire and turn two (or more) loops at that point. The pin spring can now create the tension needed to hold the pin stem in the hook. You can incorporate more loops as part of your design if you want.

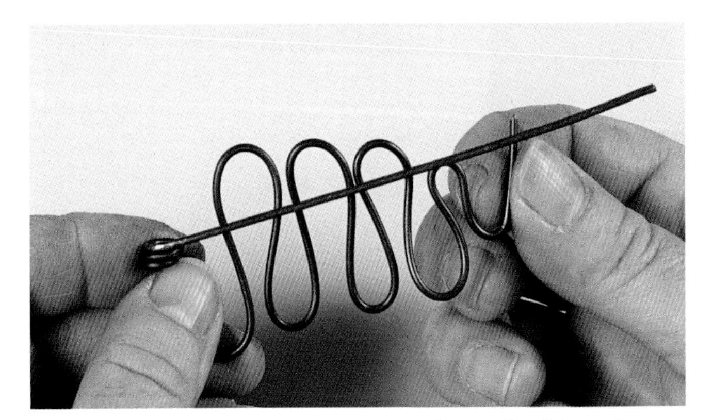

3 To make the brooch: Start at the end of the pin spring, bending and shaping the length of the wire with your fingers to form the design. (If needed, use the round-nose or flat-nose pliers to help with the smaller details.)

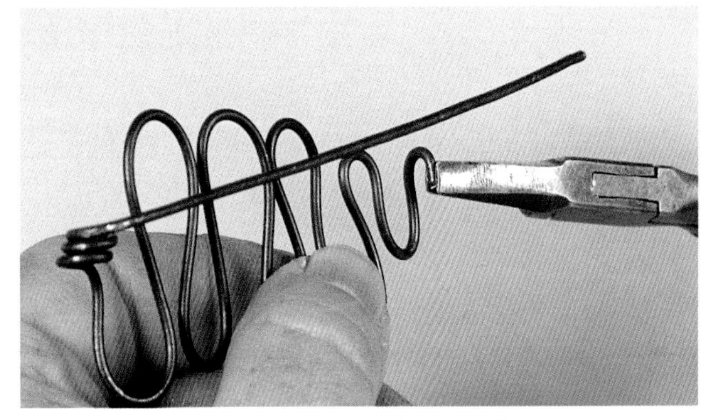

4 At the end of the design wire, use the flat-nosed pliers to shape the hook that will "catch" the pin stem.

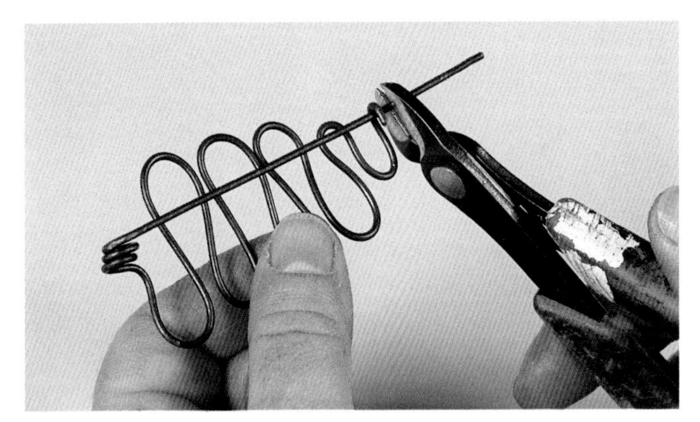

5 With the wire cutters, trim off the end of the pin stem so that it ends just past the hook when it's fastened.

6 File the end of the pin stem to a fine point and smooth it with sandpaper or an emery board. A long gradual taper works best.

Tin Star Ornaments

Working with tin cans you love adds color, pattern, and fond memories to projects made with plain wire. I love recycling the tin cans I've found while traveling or that friends have given to me. Cans with shiny elements in their designs give the ornaments extra sparkle.

YOU WILL NEED

- Tin can with printed design
- 20-gauge (.75 mm) wire, 24 inches (61 cm) in length
- Can opener
- Tin snips
- Gloves
- Sand hammer
- Regular household scissors (Don't use your best pair.)
- Sharp nail or stylus
- Round-nose pliers
- Flat-nose pliers
- Slip-joint pliers
- Bead (optional)

BEFORE YOU START

Re-read the section in Wirework Basics (page 21) on how to twist wire. You can use any color of wire for the frames, such as brass, colored copper, or plastic-coated colored wire.

1 To make the tin ornaments: With the can opener, cut off both the top and bottom of the can.

2 Using the tin snips, cut along the seam of the can. Once you've cut through the thick seam, you can use scissors for the rest of the cutting.

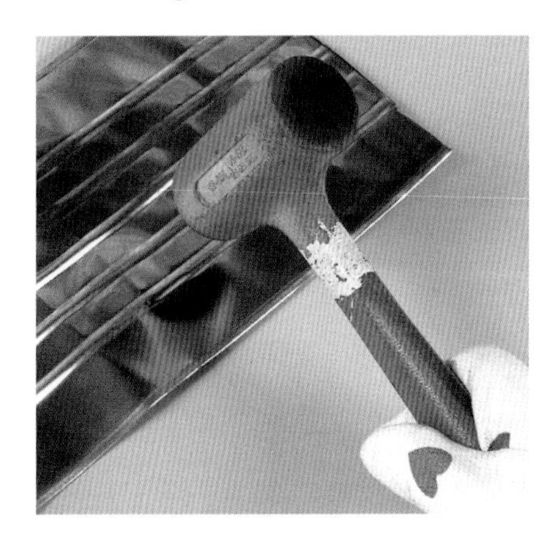

3 Wear gloves to open up the can. Be mindful of the tiny sharp slivers—they bite. Flatten the can with the sand hammer.

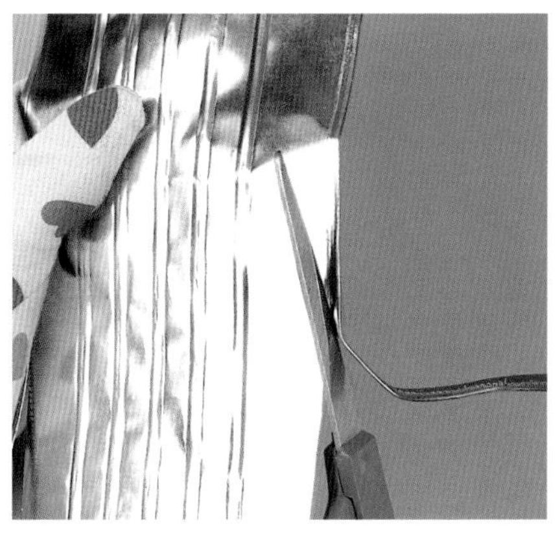

4 Once the can is open, it's easy to cut and bend. With tin snips or scissors, cut off the rims.

5 Using the sharp nail or stylus, trace a star shape for the ornament onto the tin. Cut out the shape with the scissors.

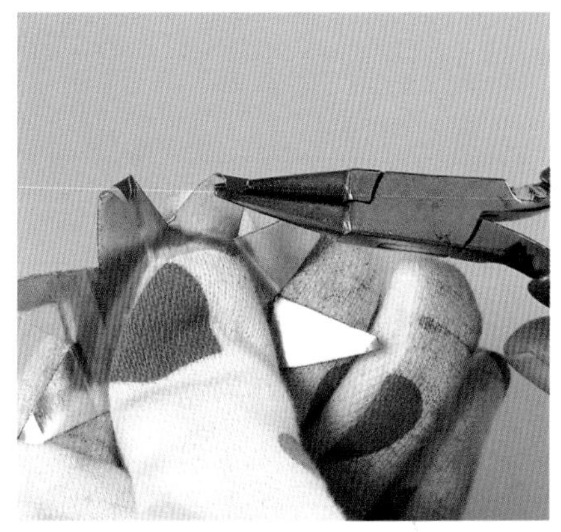

7 With the round-nose pliers, curl the tips of the star towards its back side.

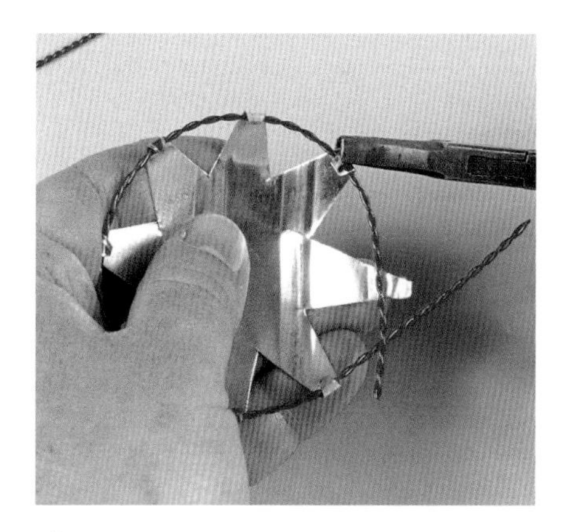

8 To make the twisted wire frame: Fold the wire in half and follow the directions on page 21 for twisting wire. You'll end up with a piece of wire that is 12 inches (30.5 cm) long. Slip the wire inside each of the curled tips of the star and crimp them closed with the flat-nose pliers.

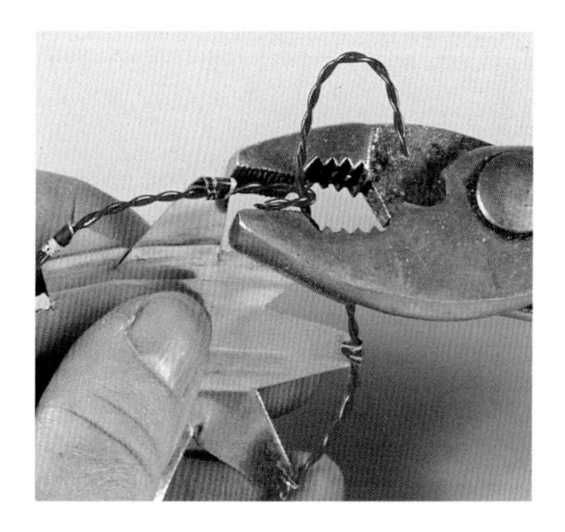

9 With the slip-joint pliers, make a hook to close one end of the wire around the other end, leaving enough wire to shape a hanging hook. As an optional final touch, you can slip a bead onto the wire.

Shiny Apples

Wadding up wire to make a shape is as easy as crumpling up a piece of paper. How much wire you need, what color you use, and your "wadding technique" will be determined by what you want to make. Large fruit and vegetables, or designs that are densely packed, require more wire. Pick a yellow wire—and go bananas!

YOU WILL NEED

20-gauge (.75 mm) red wire, 50 feet (15 m) in length

22-gauge (.64 mm) green wire, 3 feet (91.4 cm) in length

Wire cutters

Flat-nose or needle-nose pliers

BEFORE YOU START

To make shiny apples like these, I used colored copper wire. You can use plastic-coated colored wire for a different look. Copper and brass wire will look great, too.

1 To make the apples: Take the red wire and wad it up, as if you were crumpling up a piece of paper. Just keep wadding until you reach the size you want.

2 Use the last 2 or 3 feet (61 or 91.4 cm) of wire to sew through the ball and hold it together. With the flat-nose or needle-nose pliers, tuck in the straggling wily bits.

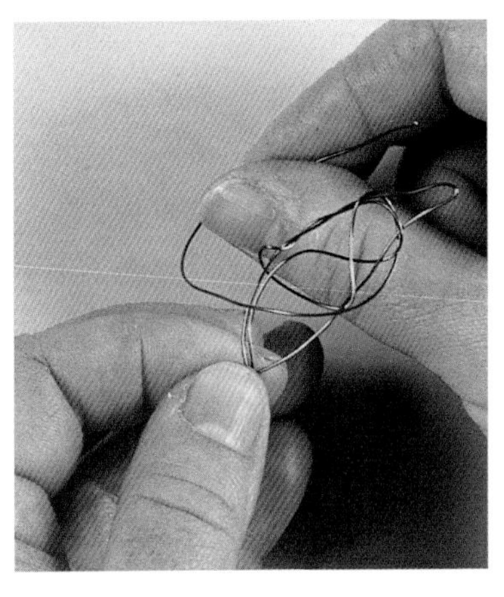

3 To make the leaves: Cut 2 feet (61 cm) of the green wire. With your hands, form a leaf shape. Wrap wire around the shape to fill it in.

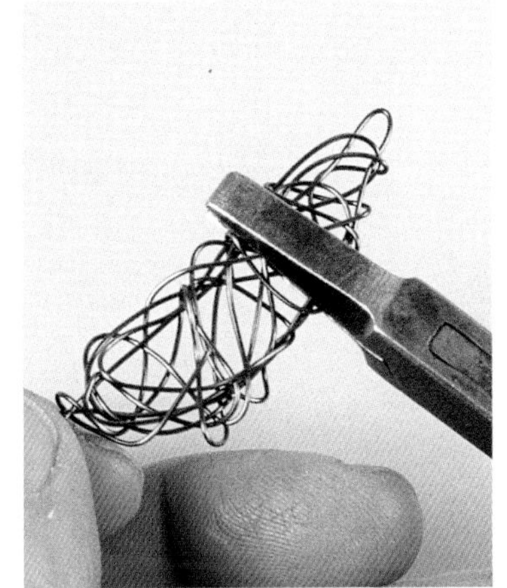

4 Use flat-nose pliers to flatten the leaf shape.

5 Using the remaining 12 inches (30.5 cm) of the green wire, tie the leaf onto the apple—twist the wire around the leaf, run it through the apple, bring it out the bottom, and tuck in the ends.

Kathleen Bolan, *Wire Wicker*, 1999, colored wire, Swarovski crystals, $2^3/_4$ x $3^1/_2$ x $3^1/_2$ in. (7.0 x 8.9 x 8.9 cm), photo by Tim Thayer

Hanging Photo Holder

I always have a few special pictures I want to look at all the time, so I designed this holder to hang above my desk. It doesn't damage the pictures, and I can change them as often as I like. You can make the rack smaller or bigger by adjusting the size of the oval ring and the number of sections. For a more elaborate design, attach a jigged pattern along the outside of the oval.

YOU WILL NEED

12-gauge (2.00 mm) steel wire, 28 inches (71.1 cm) in length

16-gauge (1.25 mm) steel wire, $11^1/_2$ feet (3.5 m) in length

24-gauge (.50 mm) steel wire, 5 feet (1.5 m) in length

$^3/_4$-inch-diameter (1.9 cm) dowel

Tape measure

Wire cutters

Wax pencil or chalk

Flat-nose pliers

Slip-joint pliers

Round-nose pliers

BEFORE YOU START

Using the tape measure and the wire cutters, cut the 16-gauge (1.25 mm) wire into the following lengths and set them aside until needed:

- 5 pieces, each 18 inches (45.7 cm) in length, for the spirals
- 5 pieces, each 9 inches (22.9 cm) in length, for the center rings

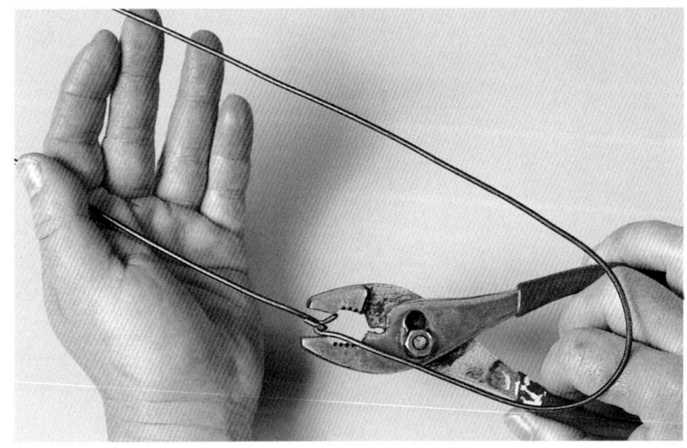

1 To make the oval base: Bend the 12-gauge (2.00 mm) steel wire into an oval ring. (Bend it so the two ends meet on the long side of the oval, where the ends will be less noticeable.) With the flat-nose pliers, bend a small hook at both ends. Crimp them together with slip-joint pliers.

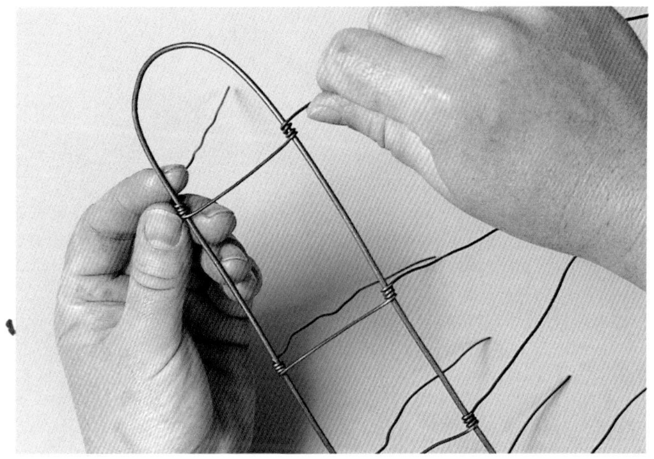

2 To make the bases of the sections: Measure off five equidistant points on both sides of the oval ring. Mark the resulting 10 points with a wax pencil or chalk. Take the five pieces of the 18-inch (45.7 cm) wire you had laid aside. Attach each wire across the oval ring at the points you marked, wrapping three to four times around each side of the oval ring. You'll end up with 10 loose ends.

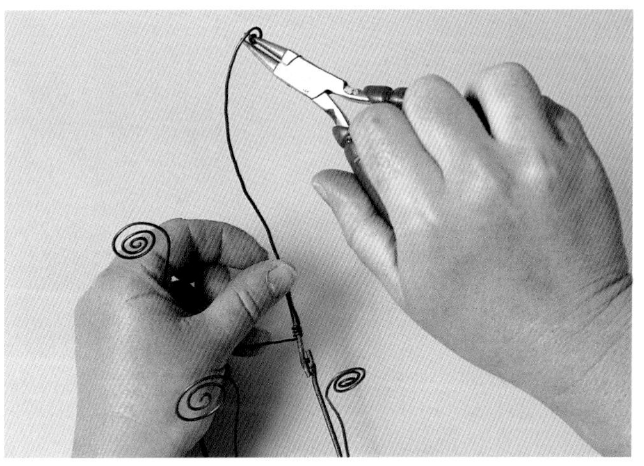

3 To make the spirals: Curl the loose ends of all 10 wires. Start each curl using the round-nose pliers. Once you've started a curl, you can continue shaping it with the flat-nose pliers or your fingers.

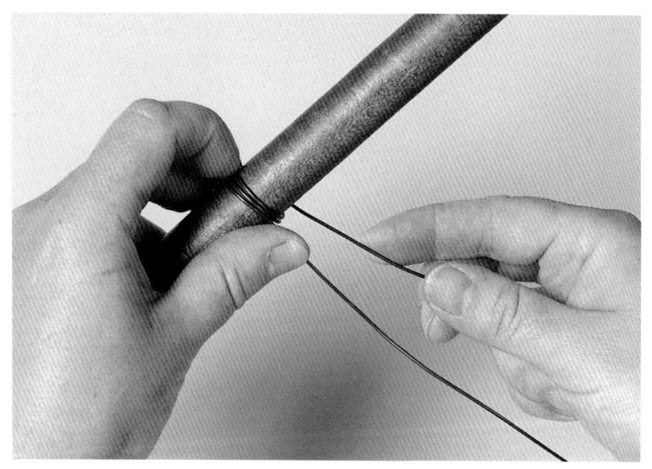

4 To make the center rings: Use the five pieces of 9-inch (22.9 cm) wire. Wrap one end of each wire three times around the dowel. Make sure the loops touch one another tightly so they'll grip the photos firmly. Remove the coils from the dowel.

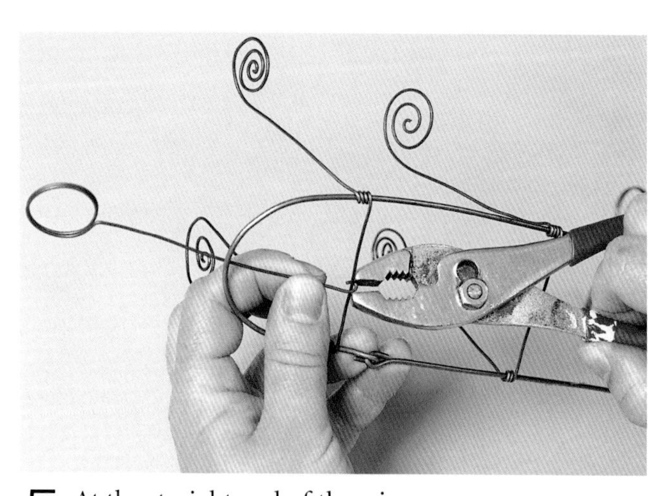

5 At the straight end of the wires you just coiled, make a small hook with the round-nose pliers. Crimp the hooks with the slip-joint pliers, attaching each of these wires to the base wires in the five sections.

6 With the 24-gauge (.50 mm) wire, tightly wrap together the three wires—the two spirals and the center ring wire—in each section.

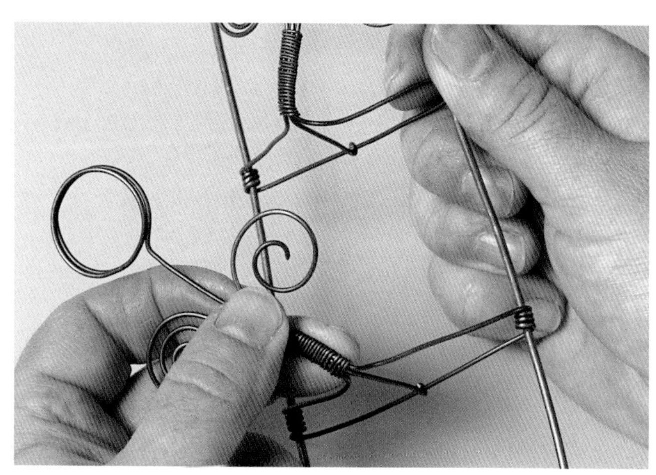

7 To finish the design, bend the wires up 90° from the point just below where you wrapped them.

Ellen Wieske/Carole Ann Fer, *Candlesticks*, 1994, clay, steel wire, various heights, photo by artist

Fancy-Free Flower Hooks

Whatever your favorite flowers and colors are, you'll have a bloomin' good time making this handy hook! Make a bunch of hooks at the same time to use up your colored scrap wires. Have fun with color combinations.

YOU WILL NEED

- 16-gauge (1.25 mm) steel wire, 32 inches (81.3 cm) long
- Plastic-coated colored wire, any gauge, at least 3 feet (91.4 cm) in length, depending on your design
- Vise
- Vise grip pliers
- Flat-nose pliers
- Round-nose pliers
- File or emery board
- Jigged piece (optional)
- Wire cutters

BEFORE YOU START

For more complex flower designs, make patterned pieces on a jig first, then stitch them on after you've formed the outside of the flower shape and wrapped it with colored wire. Also remember, pliers can damage colored wire, so you'll want to form the flower hook shape in the steel wire before you wrap it with colored wire.

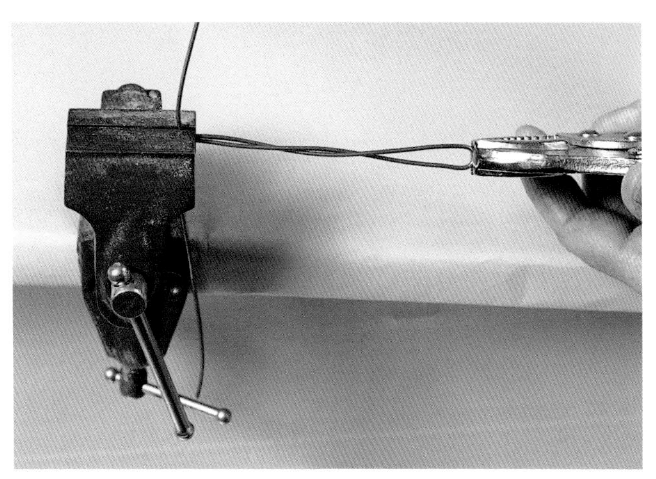

1 Bend the 16-gauge (1.25 mm) wire in half. Place the bend of the wire in the vise. Using the vise grip pliers, twist about 4 inches (10.2 cm) of the wire.

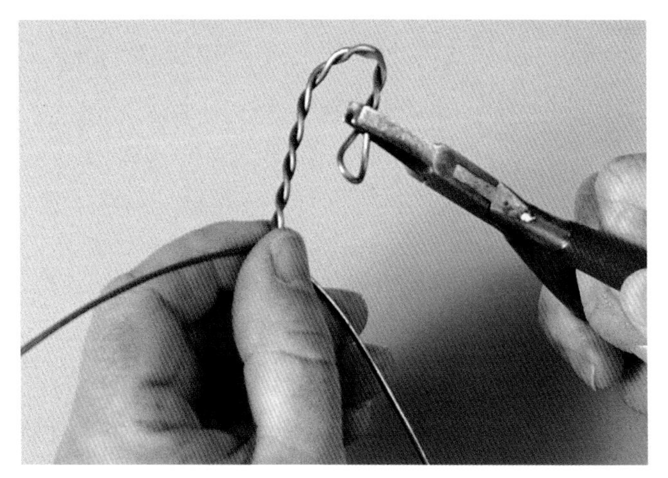

2 Using the flat-nose pliers to help, bend the twisted wire into the shape of the hook.

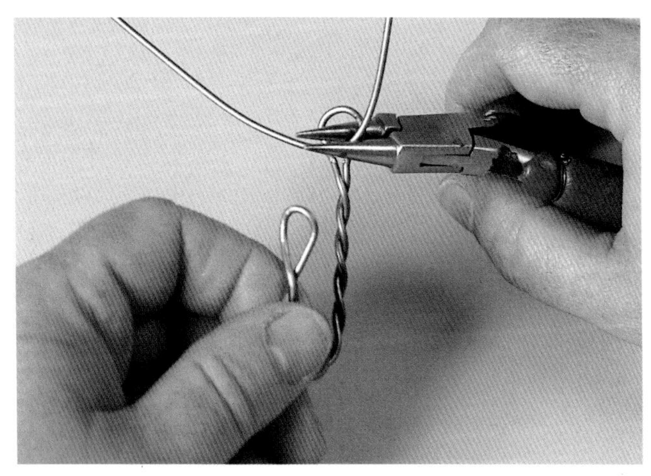

3 Position the round-nose pliers at the end of the twisted section of wire. Use the pliers to shape one of the loose ends into a loop. This is where you'll attach the hook to the wall.

4 With your fingers, form the flower shape with the untwisted ends of the wire. You may want to use the flat-nose pliers for fine detail. File the wire ends flat with the file or emery board, then butt them flush against each other.

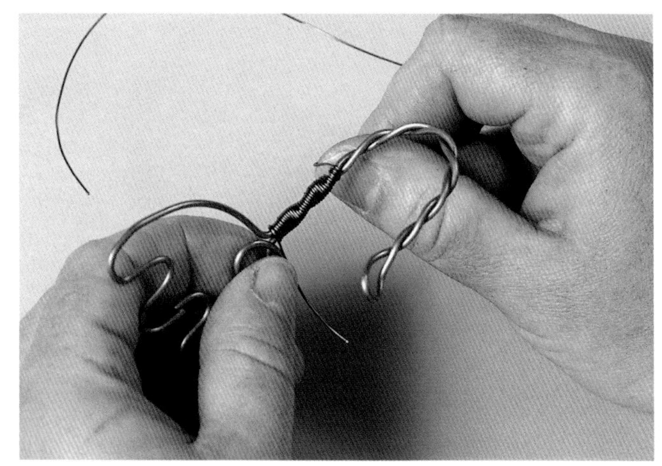

5 Wrap the hook and flower shape tightly with the colored wire. If you've made a jigged piece, stitch it on now.

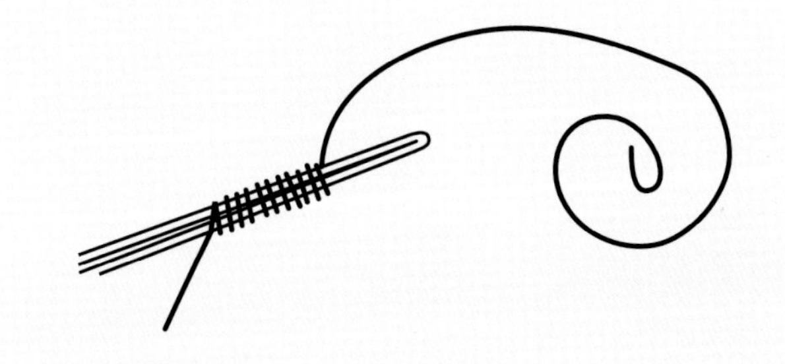

Tip: Leave a "handle" of at least 1-inch (2.5 cm) at the start of the wire. Hold onto the "handle" with one hand, while you wrap with the other hand. Cut it off later.

See-Through Mesh Box

This great-looking box lets you see what's inside, so things are always kept neat and easy to find. My favorite screen material—hardware cloth—can be found at most hardware stores, and it comes in different grid sizes. You can make the knob on the lid out of anything that can be wrapped or threaded onto a wire—seeds, beads, buttons, or charms.

YOU WILL NEED

Welded mesh hardware cloth, 1/4-inch (6 mm) grid size, cut in a square that is 12 x 12 inches (30.5 x 30.5 cm) (or 48 x 48 mesh squares)

24-gauge (.50 mm) colored wire, 13 inches (33 cm) in length

Tape measure

Regular household scissors. (Don't use your good pair.)

File

Decorative knob (Anything you can attach with wire will work.)

BEFORE YOU START

You can determine the size of hardware cloth by measuring it with a tape measure or counting the tiny squares in the mesh. Either way works. The square box measures 2 1/2 inches (6.4 cm) wide x 1 1/2 inches (3.8 cm) high (10 x 6 mesh squares). Adjust the sizes of your mesh and the lengths of wire to make smaller or bigger boxes. Be sure to use the kind of hardware cloth that is welded, not woven. The woven types tend to unravel.

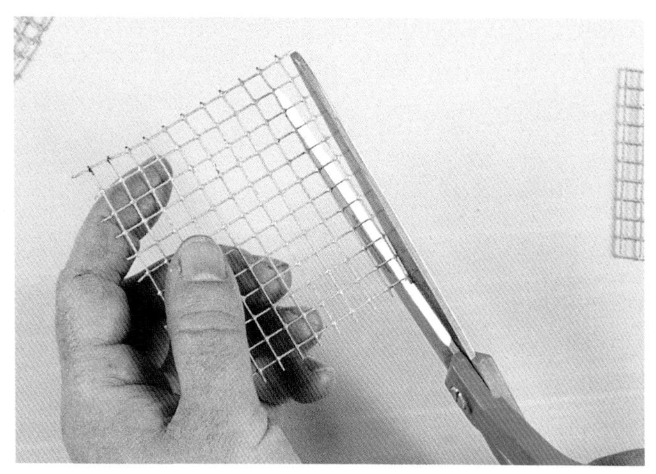

1 With the tape measure and scissors, measure and cut three pieces from the hardware cloth in the following sizes:

- For the sides of the box, cut one rectangular strip that is 1½ inches (3.8 cm) in height x 10 inches (25.4 cm) in length (or six x 40 mesh squares).
- For the two matching squares that make the lid and bottom of the box, cut two 2½-inch (6.4 cm) squares (or 10 x 10 mesh squares).

2 Cut close to the lines and file off the nubs.

Ellen Wieske, *Brooch,* 1997, sterling silver wire and ball bearings, ½ x 3 in. (1.3 x 7.6 cm), photo by artist

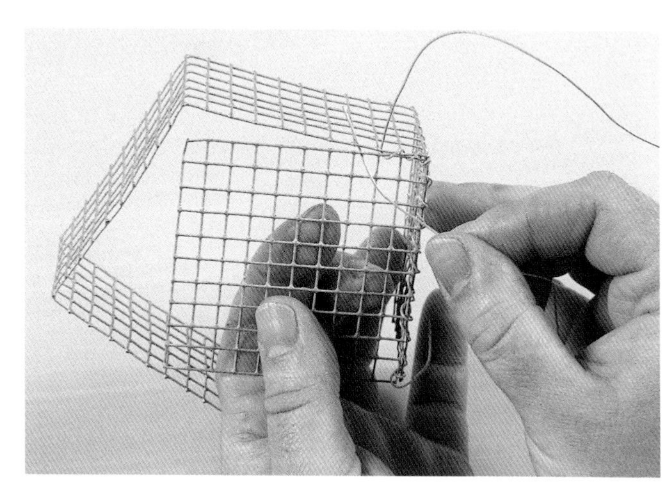

3 Bend the rectangular side piece to fit around the square bottom. With the 24-gauge (.50 mm) colored wire, stitch the two pieces together.

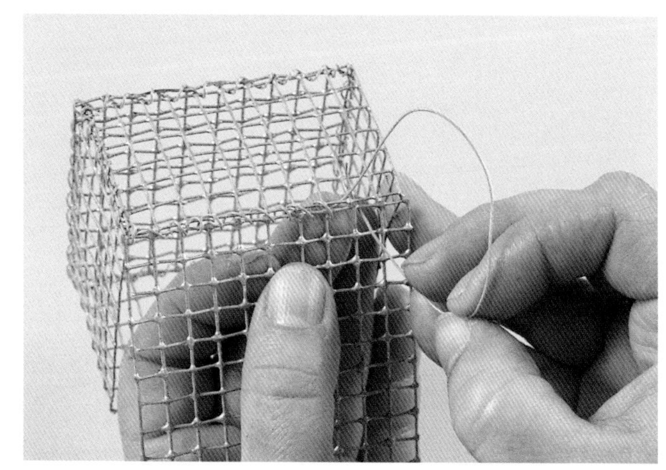

4 Stitch up the corner of the box. Then, stitch across one end of the top to create the lid. Be sure to stitch loosely so the hinge and the lid will move smoothly.

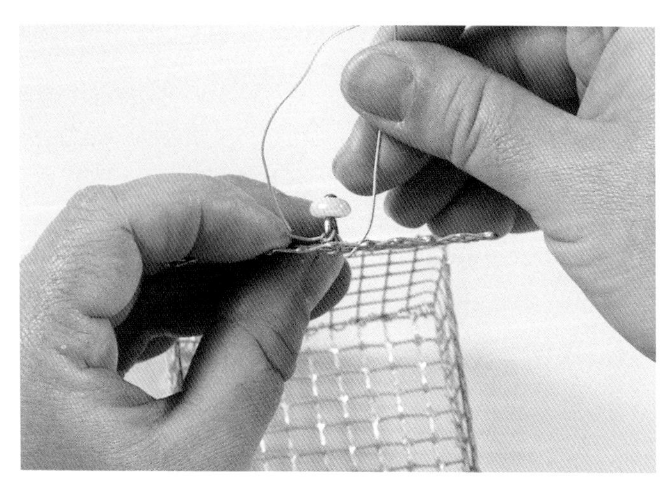

5 Tie the knob on with the wire.

Handy Catch-All Basket

Although this sturdy basket is large, it's quick and easy to make. I make these baskets every couple of months to use up my scrap wires. All those little pieces, tangled bits, or jig rejects that have accumulated in a bucket—all different sizes and colors—now have a place to go. Big baskets like this one are great for magazines and newspapers. Make a smaller version for bills or love letters.

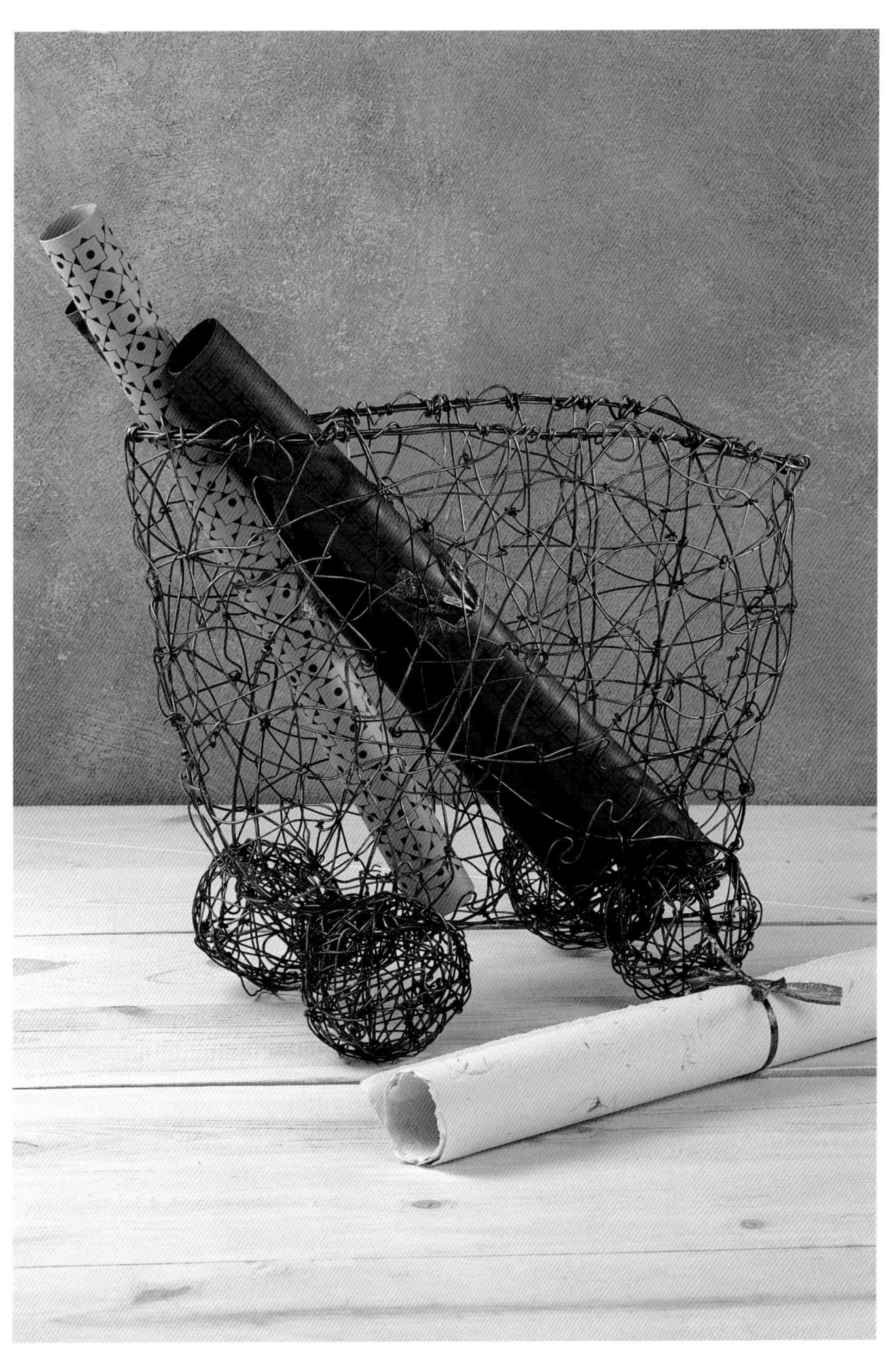

YOU WILL NEED

- Colored, steel, or brass wire—or any combination—in any gauges
- Wire cutters
- Slip-joint pliers
- Sand hammer
- Flat-nose pliers

BEFORE YOU START

The amount of wire you need will depend on the size of your basket. With its ball-feet, this basket is 16 inches (40.6 cm) long and 13 inches (33 cm) tall. Keep your wire cutters handy for frequent cutting.

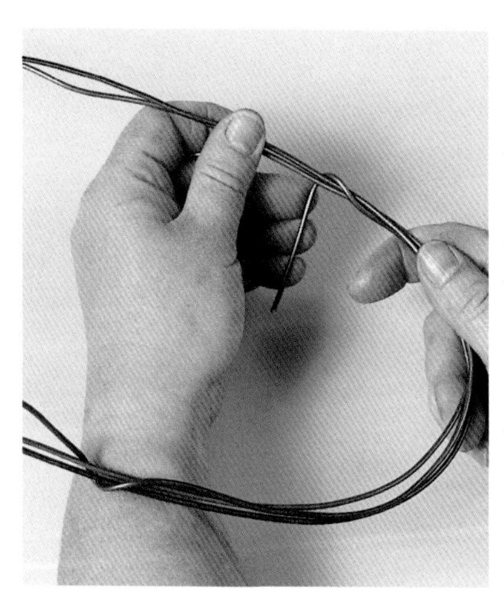

1 Using the thickest wire you can manage—several thicknesses will work well—bend the wire into an oval. Hook and crimp or wrap the wires together to make them sturdy. Use slip-joint pliers for more muscle.

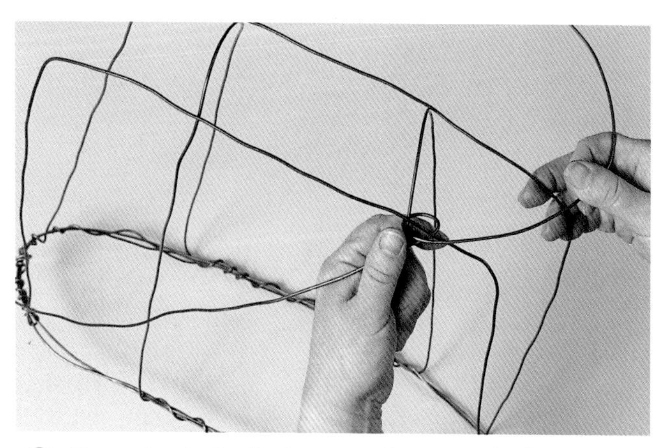

2 To make the body, just attach one end of a wire to the oval top ring by wrapping it around a few times. Then bring it down the side, across the bottom, and up the other side, and attach it to the oval top ring with a final few wraps. Attach two more wires on opposite sides of the narrow ends of the oval.

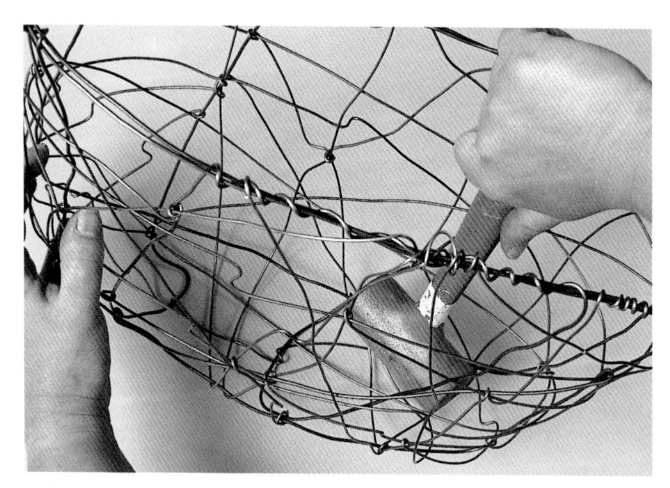

3 Weave, crimp, and wrap in more wire to build up the basket. Add it randomly until you get enough volume for the size you want. Then just push the wires into shape with the head of the sand hammer.

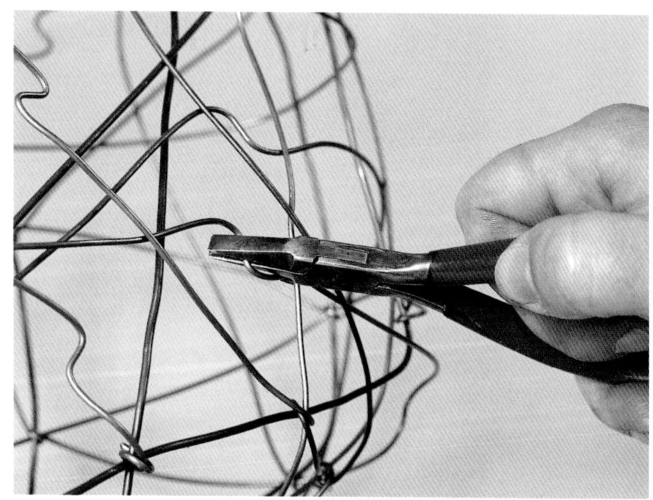

4 Use the flat-nose pliers to make "tucks" until the shape looks good.

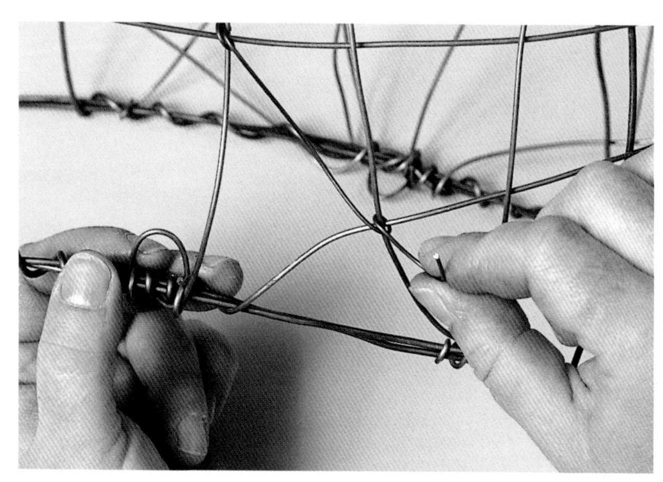

5 Add lots of thin short wires to secure and strengthen the shape.

6 To make the ball-feet, wad up any lengths of wire to make four balls of the same size. Use scrap wire to secure each ball to the bottom of the basket.

Garden Candleholder

I love candles, especially displayed in wire holders. Together they create a magic combination I never get tired of watching—light and shadow, like a moving line drawing. See for yourself—this easy-to-make holder supports a candle that will glow all night, indoors or out.

YOU WILL NEED

12-gauge (2.00 mm) steel wire, 35 inches (89 cm) in length

14-gauge (1.50 mm) steel wire. 70 inches (1.78 m) in length

16- or 18-gauge (1.25 mm or 1.00 mm) steel wire, 50 inches (1.27 m) in length

23-gauge (.57 mm) steel wire, 25 inches (63.5 cm) in length

3/4-inch-diameter (1.9 cm) dowel

3/8-inch-diameter (9.5 mm) dowel

Tape measure

Wire cutters

Flat-nose pliers

Slip-joint pliers

Wax pencil

Sand hammer

Anvil (optional)

4-inch (10.2 cm) terra-cotta planter saucer

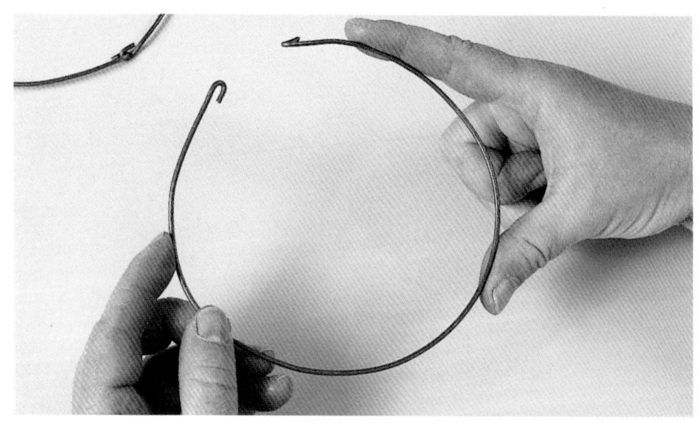

1 To make the top and bottom circles: Using the tape measure and wire cutters, measure and cut the 12-gauge (2.00 mm) wire into two lengths: one 15 inches (38.1 cm) long, and the other 20 inches (50.8 cm) long. With your fingers, bend each piece into a circle. With the flat-nose pliers, make hooks on both ends of the small circle and crimp them together with the slip-joint pliers. Repeat for the large circle.

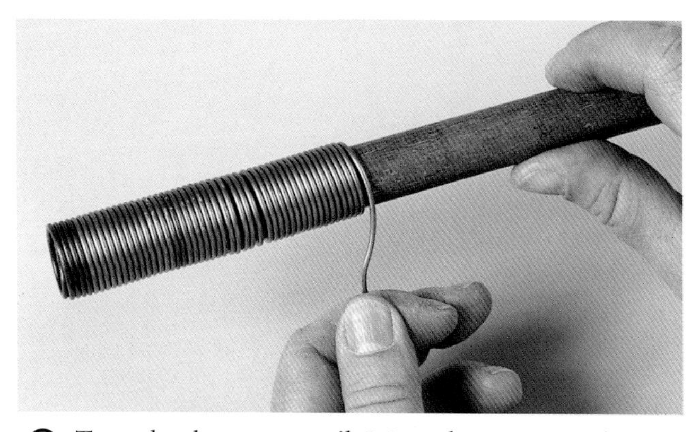

2 To make the center coil: Wrap the 14-gauge (1.50 mm) wire around the 3/4-inch-diameter (1.9 cm) dowel to create a coil that is 3 1/2 inches (8.9 cm) long.

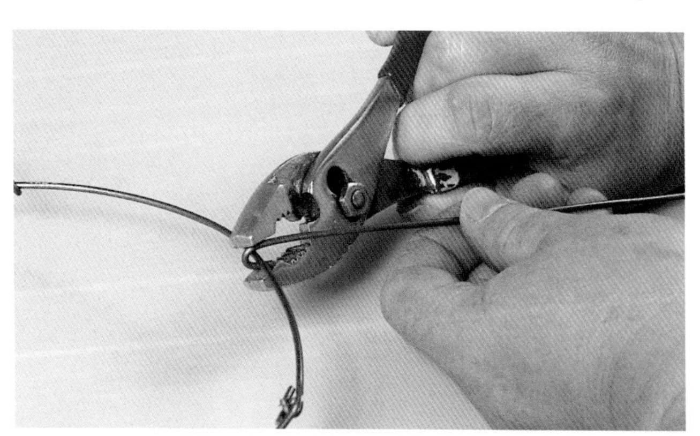

3 To make the central bundle: Cut five pieces of 14-gauge (1.50 mm) wire, each 13 inches (33 cm) long. At one end of each piece of wire, make a small hook with the flat-nose pliers. Crimp each hook onto the larger circle with slip-joint pliers.

4 With the wax pencil, mark each of the five 14-gauge (1.50 mm) wires at 3 inches (7.6 cm) from its hooked end. Then bend each wire 90° at the mark. Hold the straight length of all five of the wires together to form a tight bundle and slide the coil (that you made in step 2) over the wires.

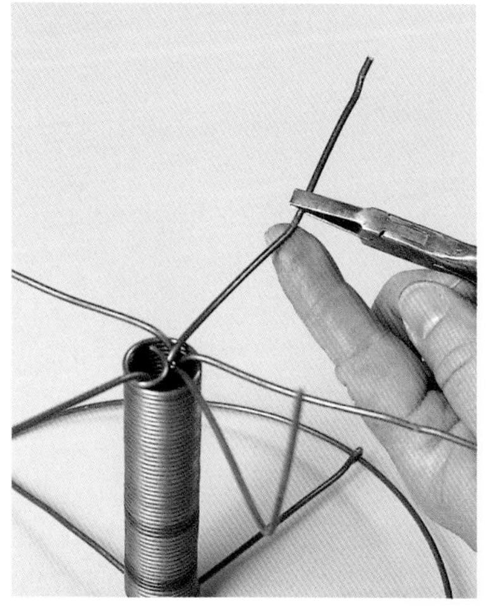

5 To make the holder for the candle dish: Take the five wires and bend each of them outward 90° at the point where the top of the coil meets them. On each wire, measure 2 1/4 inches (5.7 cm) from the coil. Position the flat-nose pliers at this mark, and bend each wire 90° up. Measure and cut the wires 1 1/2 inches (3.8 cm) above the last bend.

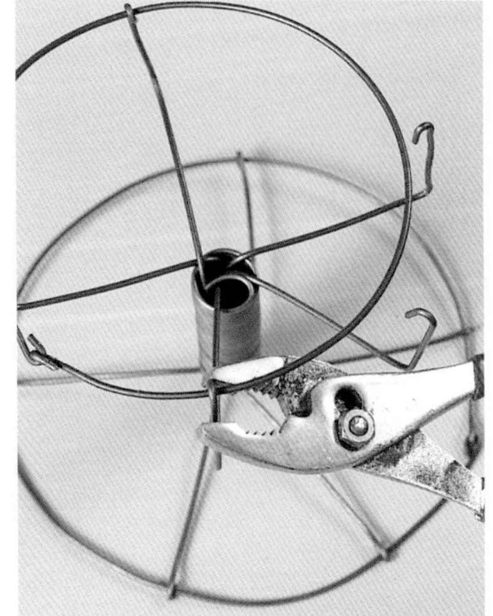

6 Using the flat-nose pliers, bend small hooks on the ends of the five wires. Attach the smaller circle to the wires by crimping each of the hooks over the circle with the slip-joint pliers.

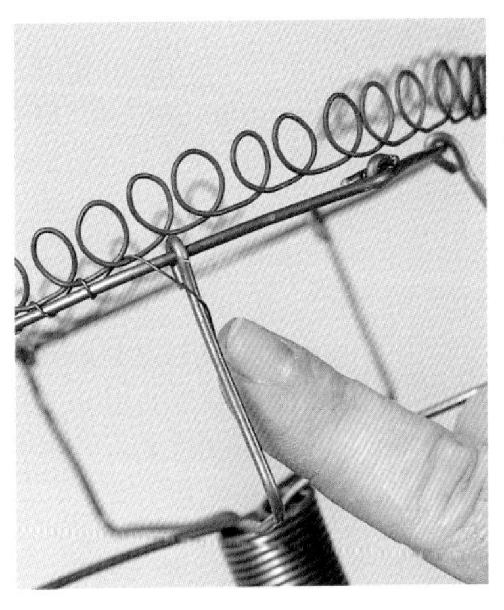

7 To make the decorative trim: Wrap the piece of 16- or 18-gauge (1.25 mm or 1.00 mm) wire around the 3/8-inch-diameter (9.5 mm) dowel to create a coil. Flatten the coil with the sand hammer on the anvil or tabletop and spread it out with your fingers. Cut the coil into two pieces to fit the top and bottom circles. Stitch the pieces onto the circles with the 23-gauge (.57 mm) wire. Slip the terra-cotta saucer through the rim to rest on top of the center coil.

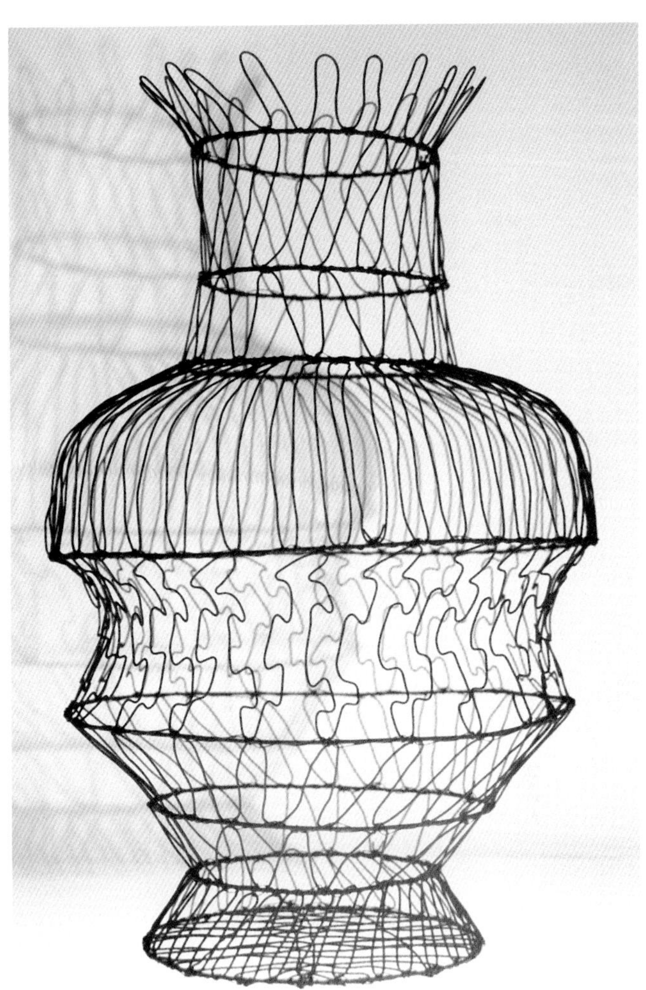

Ellen Wieske, *Vase*, 1993, steel wire, 17 x 10 in. (43.2 x 25.4 cm), photo by artist

Ellen Wieske, *Vase*, 1995, steel wire, 20 x 6 in. (50.8 x 15.2 cm), photo by artist

Ellen Wieske, *Candlesticks*, 1996, steel wire, 20 x 9 in. (50.8 x 22.9 cm), photo by artist

Round Trivet

This project is one I teach to beginners in my workshop to demonstrate how much fun it is to work on a jig. It's wonderful to make because the steps are simple, and there is tremendous room for variation. No two trivets ever look alike. They can be large or small—to hold a Thanksgiving turkey or a tea cup.

BEFORE YOU START

The copper trivet is 5 inches (12.7 cm) in diameter, with three pieces of jigged patterns. How much wire you need and how many patterns you'll use will be determined by how big you want your trivet to be. You can also use steel or brass wire, as shown in the other examples below.

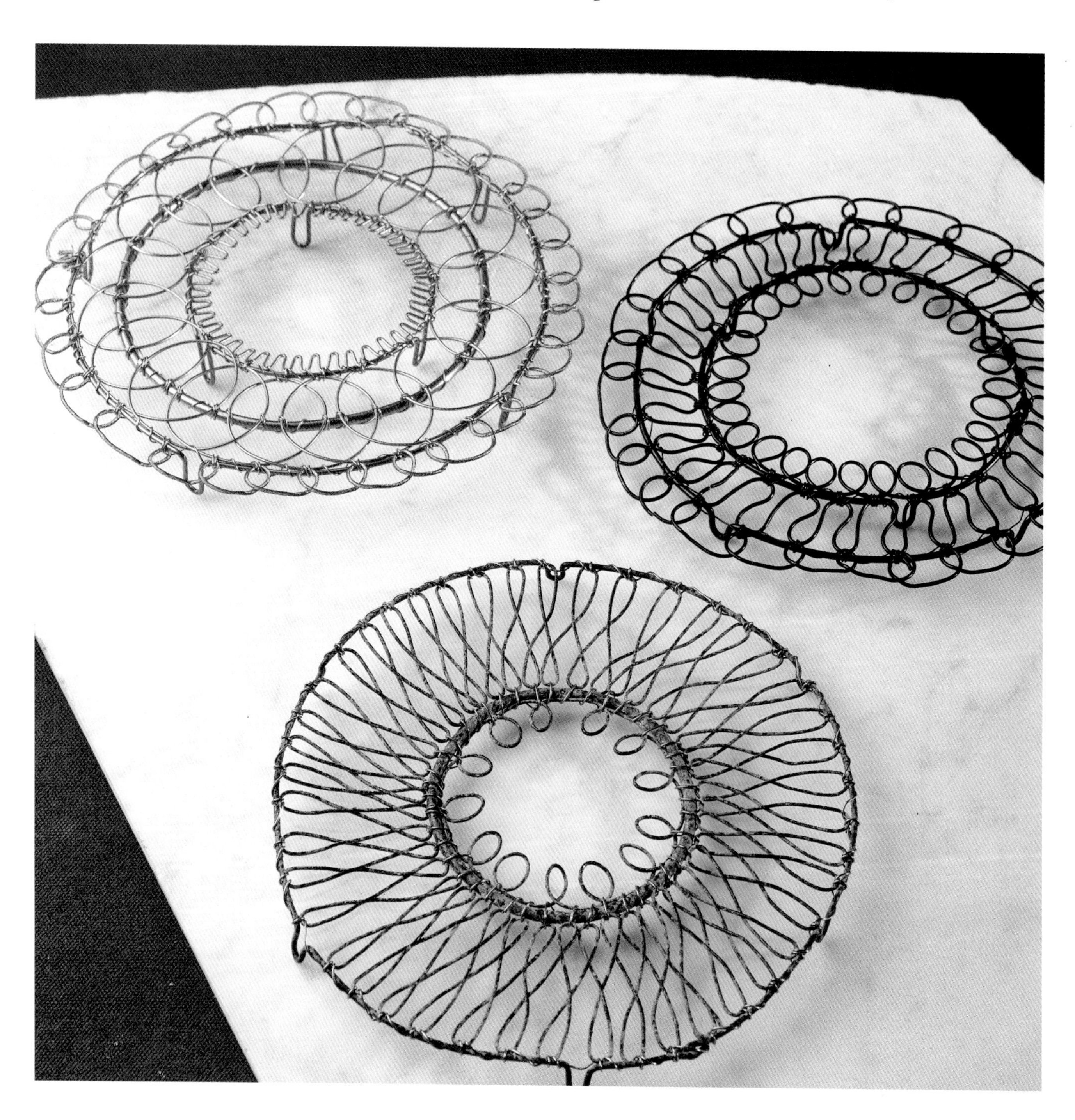

YOU WILL NEED
14-gauge (1.50 mm) copper wire, 6 feet (1.83 m) in length
18-gauge (1.00 mm) copper wire, 40 feet (12.2 m) in length
24-gauge (.50 mm) copper wire, 20 feet (6.1 m) in length
Flat jig, fixed or adjustable
Wire cutters
Tape measure
Slip-joint pliers

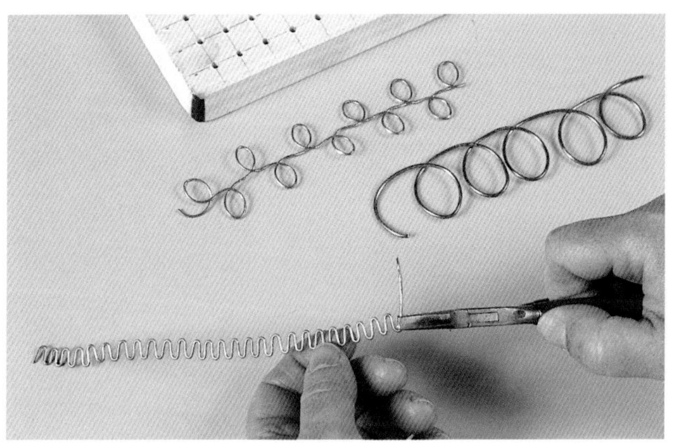

1 To make the design parts of the trivet: Use the 18-gauge (1.00 mm) wire and the jig to create different patterns that will result in 2-foot (5.1 cm) lengths. Make some narrow patterns, some wide. Have fun!

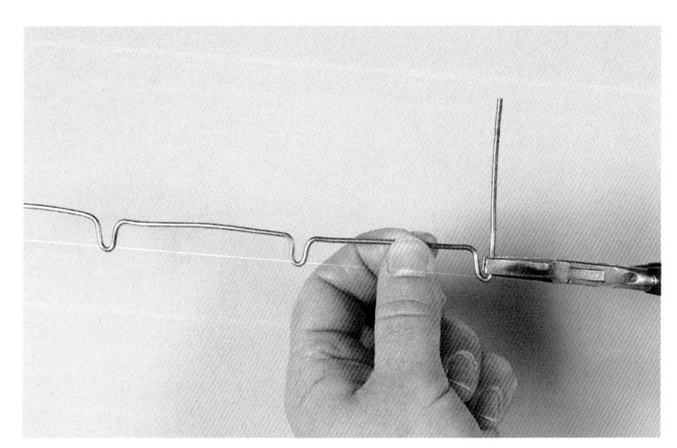

2 To make the frame strip: Measure 2 inches (5.1 cm) from the end of the 14-gauge (1.50 mm) wire and bend a U-shaped trivet-foot at that point. Bend more trivet feet down the rest of the wire, spacing them about 2 inches (5.1 cm) apart.

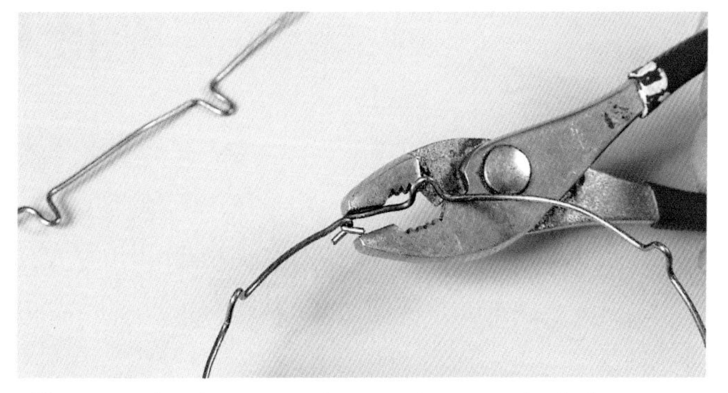

3 To make the center frame: Cut an 8-inch-long (20.3 cm) piece of the frame strip. Bend it into a circle. Make hooks on each end and crimp the two hooks together with the slip-joint pliers. For now, lay aside the rest of the frame strip.

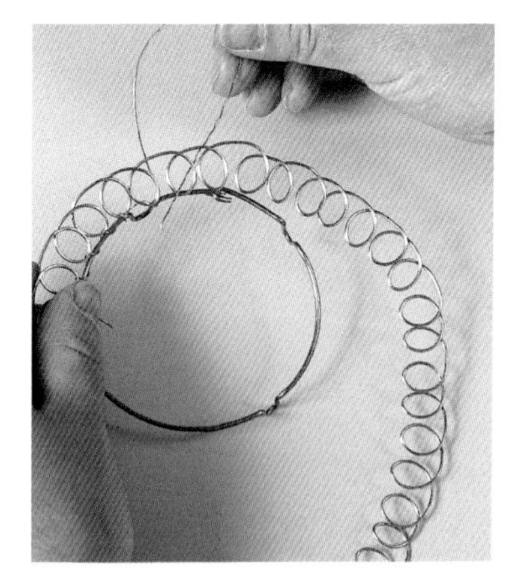

4 Using the 24-gauge (.50 mm) wire, stitch one of the patterns you made on the jig onto the round center frame. Cut off any extra wire. Tip: Use scrap wire to help hold the parts in place until you've stitched them.

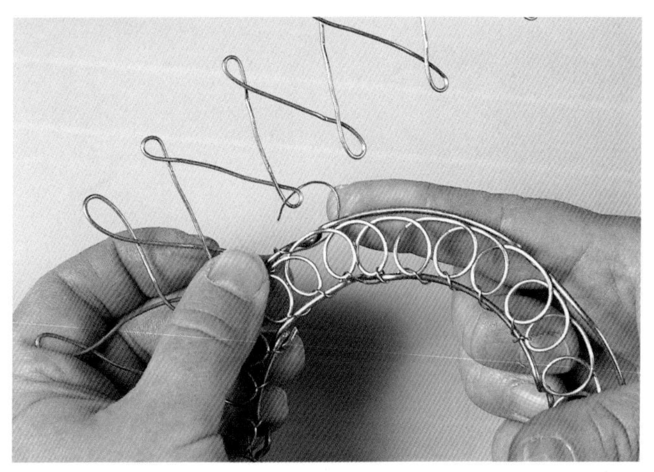

5 To increase the size of the trivet and the complexity of its design, merely add on more frames and patterns. Use the frame strip you made in step 2 and bend it around the parts you've already stitched together to determine how much of it you will need next. (If necessary, make additional frame strips.) Pick another pattern. Stitch the new pattern and the second frame onto the central piece. Repeat until you've made the size trivet you want.

Wild Flowers

How many flowers in one vase? What color wires to use? What shape flowers or leaves? What lengths to make the stems? What gauge wire to use? Whatever questions you might have, the answers will always be right—these wild flowers don't have any rules! This is a great project for using up short bits of leftover wire from either your jig practicing or other projects.

YOU WILL NEED

(FOR ONE 12-INCH [30.5 CM] FLOWER)

14- or 18-gauge (1.50 mm or 1.00 mm) wire, 2 feet (61 cm) in length, for the stem wire

18- or 20-gauge (1.00 mm or .75 mm), 2 to 4 feet (1.22 m) in length, depending on your petal pattern

23-gauge (.57 mm) wire, 3 feet (91.4 cm) in length

Flat jig or dowel

Flat-nose pliers

Slip-joint pliers

BEFORE YOU START

The size and amount of wire you need depends on the design of your flower and how tall you want it to be. The flower in this project is 12 inches (30.5 cm) tall. I used black steel wire for the flower, leaves, and stem, but you can use any kind and color of wire—or any combination.

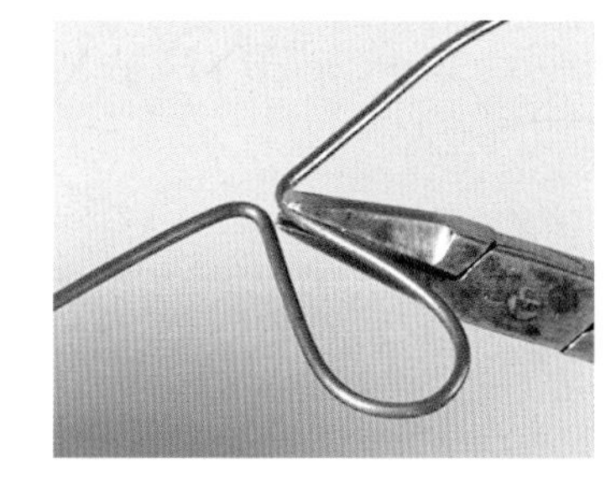

1 To make the leaf on the stem wire: At 9 inches (22.9 cm) from the end of the 2-foot (61 cm) length of wire, use the flat-nose pliers to bend a leaf shape.

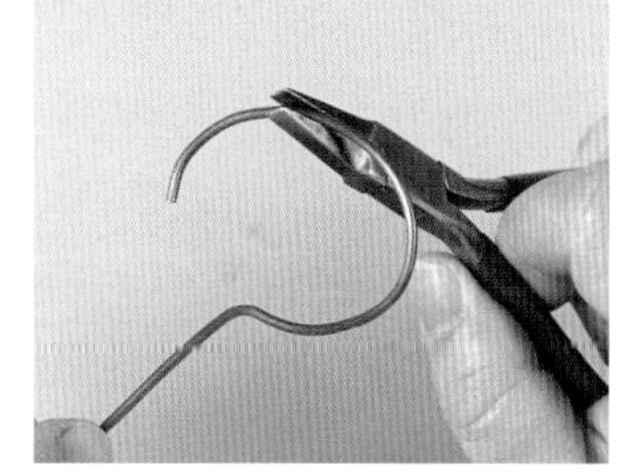

2 To make the center of the flower: Use the flat-nose pliers to bend a circle at the end of the stem wire.

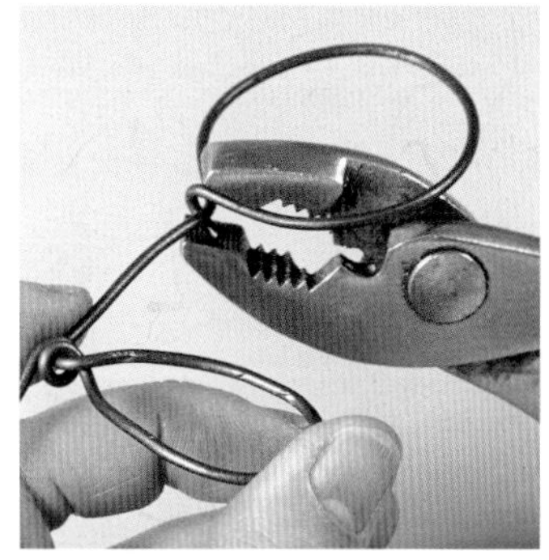

3 At the end of the flower center you just formed, make a small hook with the flat-nose pliers and crimp it onto the stem wire with the slip-joint pliers. This will keep the flower center secured to the stem wire.

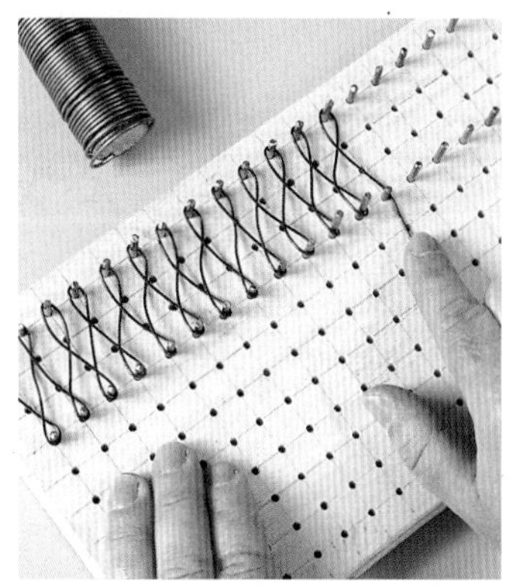

4 To make the petals: Depending on your design, use the 18- or 20-gauge (1.00 mm or .75 mm) wire to make a pattern on your flat jig or dowel. Use any pattern or size as long as you make enough to go around your flower center.

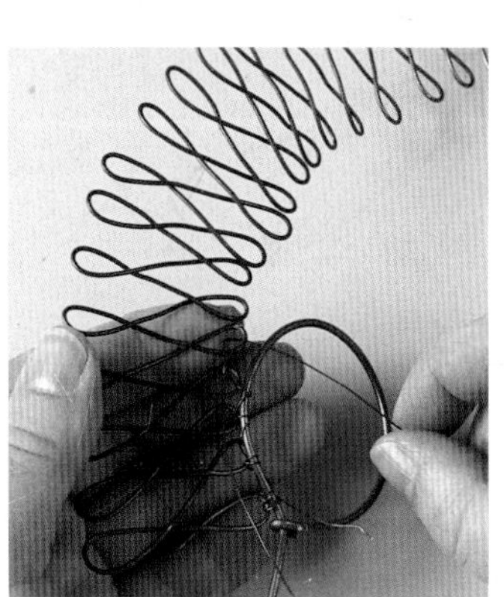

5 Wrap the petals onto the center loop with the 23-gauge (.57 mm) wire.

Tip: When you put the flowers into a vase, use sand or cat litter to help support them.

Wired-Up Mug

Transform an ordinary drinking glass by wiring on a fancy handle. Choose a footed glass with an indentation above the foot, so the wire won't slip off. Mix and match colored wire for holiday parties. Or use shiny brass wire to glow with a candlelit dinner.

YOU WILL NEED

14-gauge (1.50 mm) brass or steel wire, 20 inches (50.8 cm) in length

20-gauge (.75 mm) brass or colored wire, 80 inches (1.9 m) in length, cut into three pieces of 26 inches (66 cm) each

Flat-nose pliers

Slip-joint pliers

BEFORE YOU START

How much wire you'll need for the handle depends on the size of your glass. A 4-inch-tall (10.2 cm) glass was used for this project. Taller glasses will require more wire. Cut the long piece of 20-gauge wrapping wire into shorter pieces to make the wrapping easier.

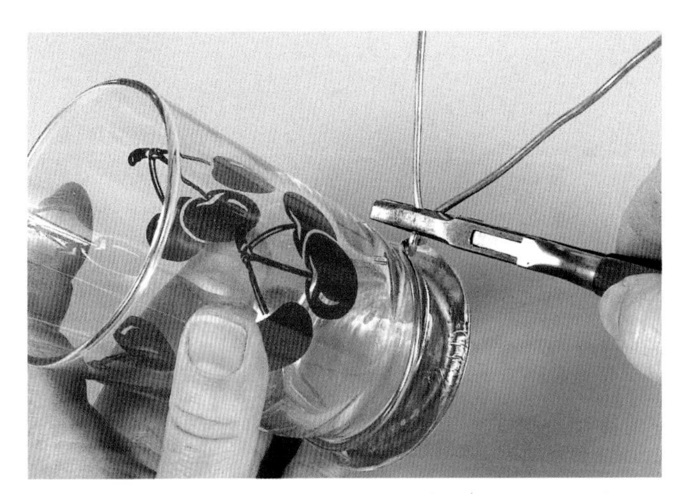

1 Center the 14-gauge (1.50 mm) wire around the base of the glass. With the flat-nose pliers, tightly twist the two lengths of wires two or three times to secure them to the base of the glass. Then make small hooks at the loose ends of the wires.

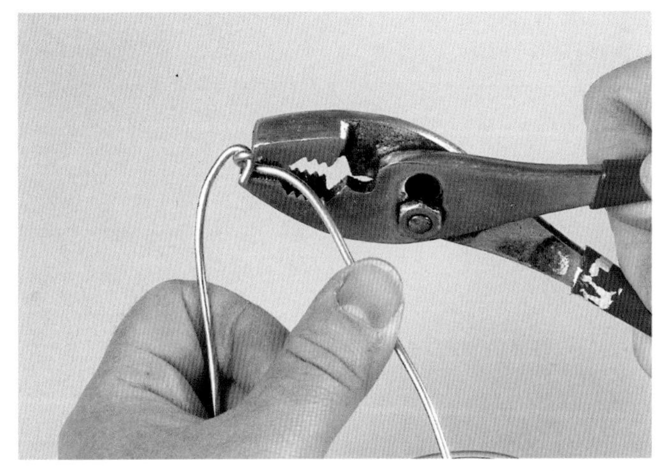

2 With the slip-joint pliers, lock the wire ends together by crimping the hooks together.

3 Using your fingers, bend the wire into a simple, curved handle shape.

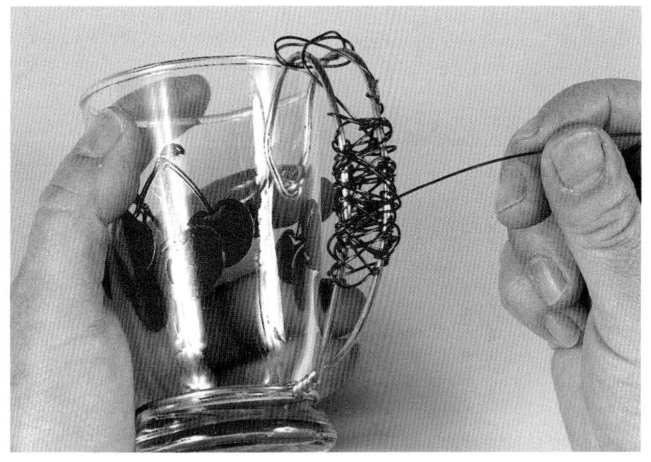

4 Wrap the handle with the 20 gauge (.75 mm) wire pieces. Tuck in any sharp, pointy ends.

5 Bend the handle against the glass so that it stays there firmly. Here's how: Push the handle straight against the glass, then push it *way* to the right—and then *way* to the left. This creates tension between the handle and the glass. Finally, center the handle on the glass.

CARE TIP

If you use steel wire that might rust, either go with it and let it rust (I did), or dry the handle immediately after washing, and rub it with oil.

Bright and Brassy Necklace Holder

Show off your favorite necklaces and keep them neat with this attractive holder. Make other holders to organize lots of other things—keys, measuring spoons, dog leashes—you name it!

YOU WILL NEED

- 12-gauge (2.00 mm) brass wire, 45 inches (1.1 m) in length
- 16-gauge (1.25 mm) brass wire, 4 feet (1.2 m) in length
- 18-gauge (1.00 mm) brass wire, 5 feet (1.5 m) in length
- 24-gauge (.50 mm) brass wire, 4 feet (1.22 m) in length
- Tape measure
- Flat-nose pliers
- Wire cutters
- Flat jig, fixed or adjustable
- 1/4-inch-diameter (6 mm) dowel
- Sand hammer
- Anvil (optional)

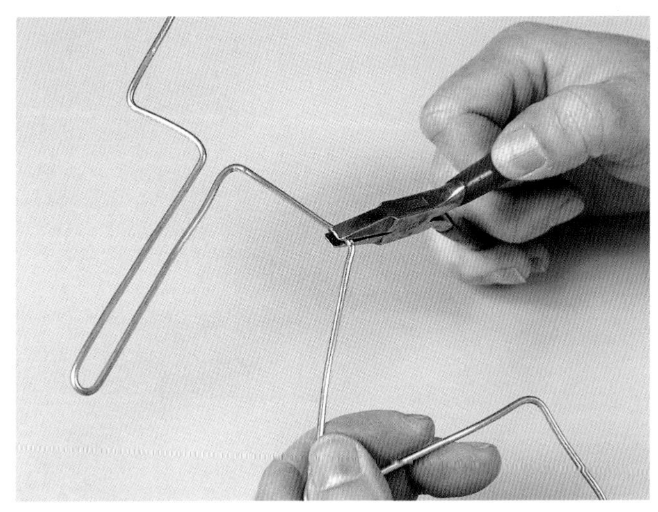

1 To make the hooks: With the tape measure and the flat-nose pliers, measure and bend the 12-gauge (2.00 mm) wire to match the dimensions in figure 1. Work from the left side of the holder to its right.

- At $3\frac{1}{2}$ inches (8.9 cm), bend the wire 90°.
- At $1\frac{1}{2}$ inches (3.8 cm) from the previous bend, make a 90° bend.
- At 1 inch (2.5 cm) from the previous bend, make a 90° bend in the opposite direction.
- At 3 inches (7.6 cm) from the previous bend, make a U-shape with the long end of the wire.
- Continue down the length of the wire, using your tape measure and the flat-nose pliers until you've made four hooks.

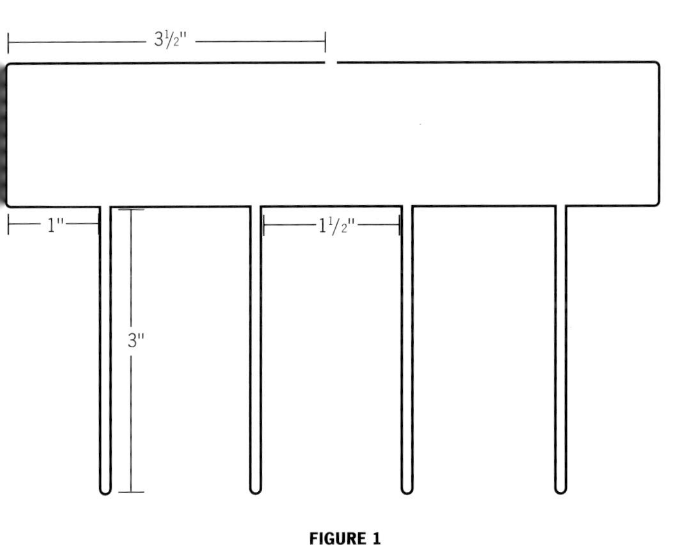

FIGURE 1

2 To make the right side and top: Measure another $1\frac{1}{2}$ inches (3.8 cm) along the wire to make the right side of the holder. Then, using the flat-nose pliers, bend the wire up 90° so that the ends of both wires meet at the top, forming a rectangle. With the wire cutters, trim off any excess wire as needed.

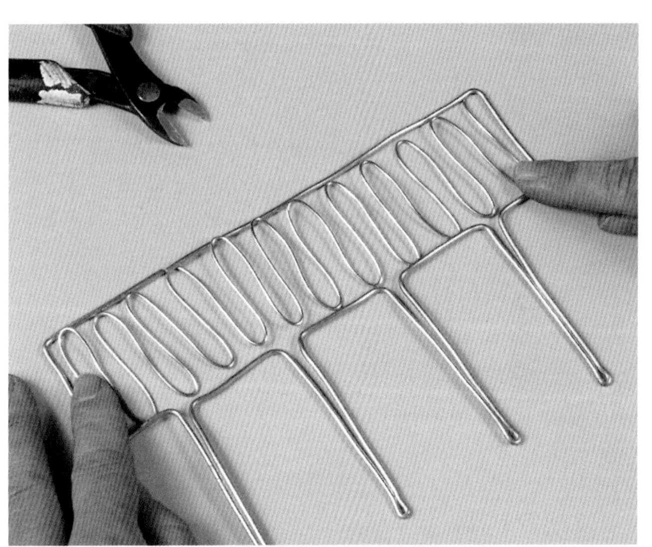

3 To make the center design: Set up the jig to measure intervals of $\frac{1}{4}$ x $1\frac{1}{2}$ inches (6 mm x 3.8 cm). Use the 16-gauge (1.25 mm) wire and make enough of the pattern to fit inside the frame.

4 To make the decorative trim: Wrap the 18-gauge (1.00 mm) wire around the dowel to make the pattern. Remove the wire from the dowel. Using the sand hammer, flatten the wire pattern on the anvil or tabletop. Then spread the loops with your fingers.

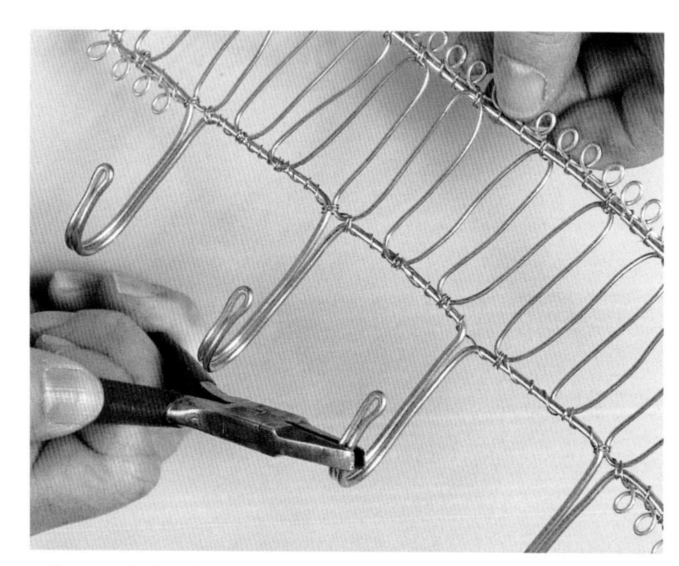

6 With the flat-nose pliers, bend the hooks up into their final position, so you can hang things from them.

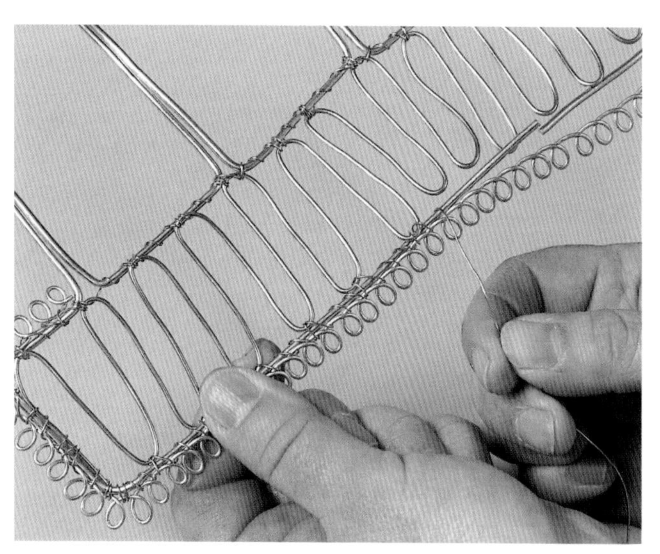

5 With the 24-gauge (.50 mm) wire, stitch the wire pattern to the frame.

Kathleen Bolan, *Untitled*, 2000, sterling silver wire bracelet with handmade lampworked glass bead with silver leaf, 27 in. (68.6 cm), photo by Tim Thayer

Looped Earrings

Both the loop size, and the thickness or color of wire you pick, will affect the look of these earrings. The variations are practically endless. For the health of your ears, I always recommend making the ear wires out of sterling silver, or plated wire in silver or gold.

YOU WILL NEED

(FOR EACH PAIR OF EARRINGS)

- 18-gauge (1.00 mm) silver, brass, or colored wire, 3 feet (.91 m) in length
- 3/8-inch-diameter (9.5 mm) dowel
- Sand hammer
- Anvil or smooth piece of steel
- Wire cutters
- Round-nose pliers
- Flat-nose pliers
- Emery board or file

(FOR EACH PAIR OF EAR WIRES)

- 20-gauge (.75 mm) sterling silver, plated silver, or plated gold wire, 4 inches (10.2 cm) in length
- Steel hammer with a polished or smooth face

BEFORE YOU START

The earrings in this project are small, about 1 inch (2.5 cm) in diameter, with tiny loops. To make earrings with larger loops, just use a larger dowel. If you wish, you can buy ready-made ear wires at jewelry supply or craft stores.

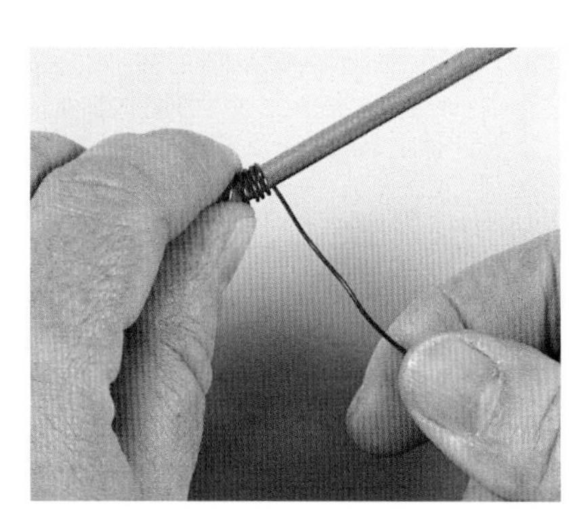

1 To make the earrings: wrap all of the 18-gauge (1.00 mm) wire around the dowel, making a spring.

2 Use the sand hammer against the anvil or the smooth piece of steel to flatten the spring.

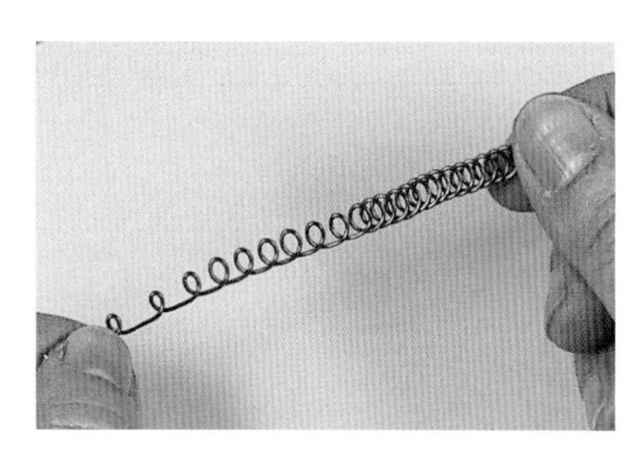

3 Spread out the flattened spring with your fingers.

4 With the wire cutters, cut off 15 loops for each earring. Bend the 15 loops into a circle. Overlap the two end loops—the ear wire attaches through these two loops. (If you've bought ear wires, attach one to each of the earrings with the flat-nose pliers now. See step 8.)

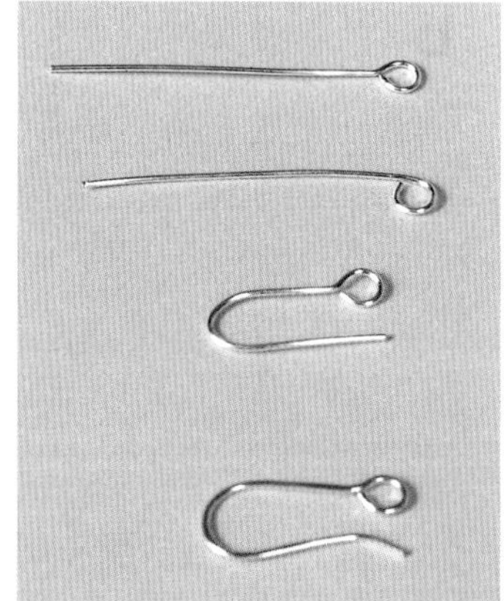

5 To make the ear wires: With the wire cutters, cut the silver wire in half, making two pieces, each 2 inches (5.1 cm) long. Then shape each piece in the sequence as shown in the photo to the left:

- With the round-nose pliers, make a small loop at one end of the wire.
- Using flat-nose pliers, center the loop on the wire.
- With your fingers, bend the wire into a U-shape.
- With the flat-nose pliers, bend the straight end away from the looped end.

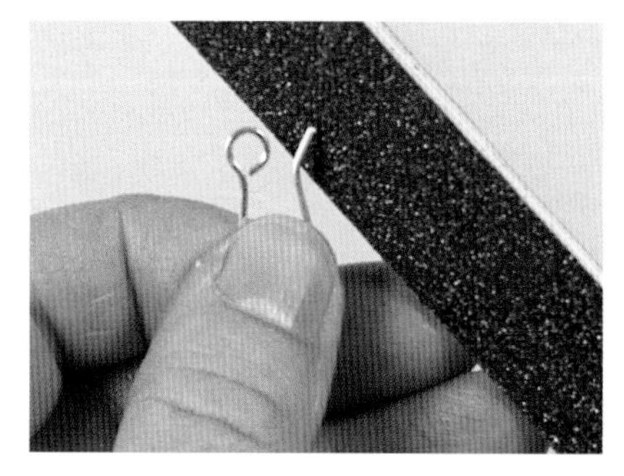

6 With the emery board, smooth the bent point.

7 To strengthen the soft silver wire, flatten it against an anvil or smooth piece of steel, using the polished steel hammer.

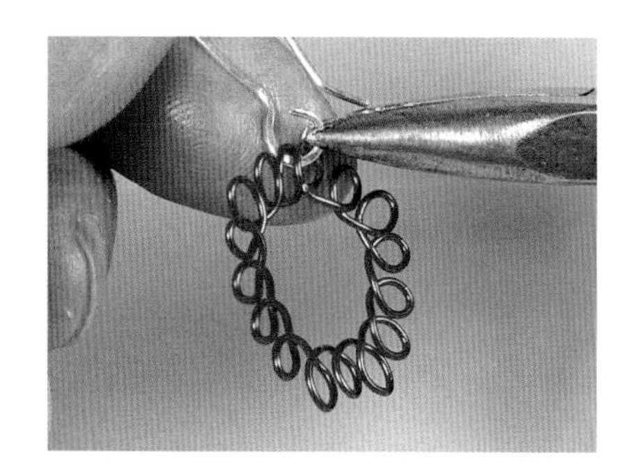

8 Attach the ear wire to the earring with the flat-nose pliers.

Bread Lover's Bread Basket

This version of a French country farm basket is both elegant and practical. You can make baskets in any size and shape to match your bread—long and deep for a baguette, or round for foccacia, bagels or hot rolls. It will be just as beautiful filled with fresh fruit and vegetables.

YOU WILL NEED

- 1/8-inch (3 mm) aluminum wire, 40 feet (12.2 m) in length
- 1/4-inch (6 mm) aluminum wire, 7 feet (2.13 m) in length
- 18- or 20-gauge (1.00 or .75 mm) plastic-coated colored wire, 20 feet (6.1 m) in length
- 23- or 24-gauge (.57 or .50 mm) scrap wire, lengths as needed
- Adjustable flat jig
- 3/4-inch-diameter (1.9 cm) dowel
- Tape measure
- Wire cutters
- File
- Sand hammer
- Anvil or smooth piece of steel
- Needle-nose pliers

BEFORE YOU START

Look over the section in Wirework Basics (page 18) on making patterns on flat wooden jigs. The bottom of this basket measures $3\frac{1}{2}$ inches (8.9 cm) wide and 13 inches (33 cm) long. At the top it's 16 inches (40.6 cm) long. Adjust wire lengths to match the size of your basket. Keep the tape measure handy to measure each length of wire before you cut it.

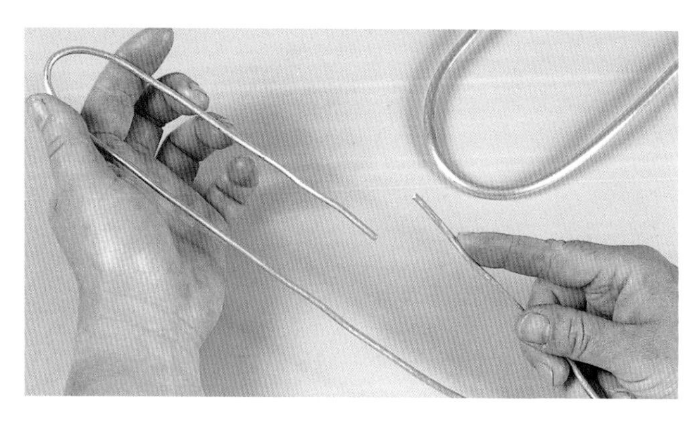

1 To make the three rims: Use your fingers to shape and bend three aluminum wire oval rings. File the ends square and butt the ends of the wire together.

- Cut the $\frac{1}{4}$-inch (6 mm) wire to a length of 41 inches (104 cm) to make the top oval.
- The remaining 33 inches (83.8 cm) of the $\frac{1}{4}$-inch (6 mm) wire is the outside bottom ring.
- Cut the $\frac{1}{8}$-inch (3 mm) wire to a length of 27 inches (68.6 cm) to make the inside center bottom oval.

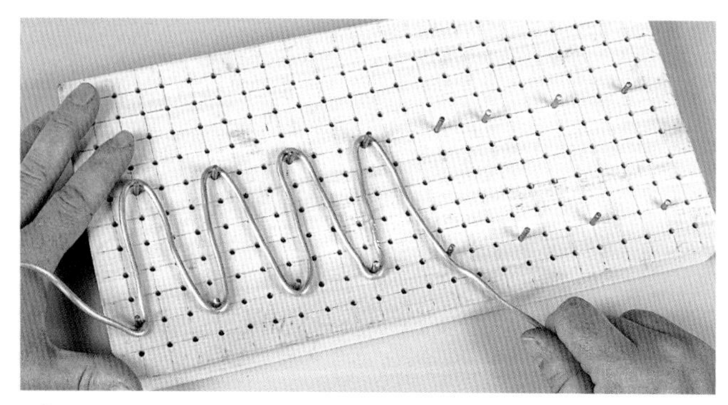

2 To make the side piece: Set up your jig at intervals of 1 x $2\frac{1}{2}$ inches (2.5 x 6.4 cm). Cut the $\frac{1}{8}$-inch (3 mm) aluminum wire to a length of 15 feet (4.6 m), and bend it around the jig nails, counting 24 times on one side—48 bends in all. Remove the piece from the jig. Using your fingers, stretch out the jigged pattern and adjust it to make sure it fits both on the bottom outside oval and the top oval.

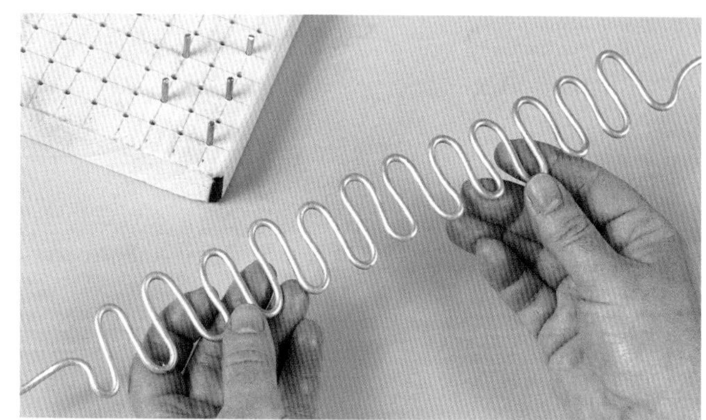

3 To make the center pattern for the bottom: Set new intervals on the jig: 1 x 1 inch (2.5 x 2.5 cm). Make another cut of the $\frac{1}{8}$-inch (3 mm) wire, $3\frac{1}{2}$ feet (1.1 m) in length. Leaving 2 inches (5.1 cm) of the wire free at the start of the wire, bend the rest of the wire 15 times, and then leave 2 more inches (5.1 cm) free on the other end. After final shaping in steps 7 and 8, this piece will have 17 loops. (See figure 1.)

4 To make the two coiled pieces: Cut a piece of the $\frac{1}{8}$-inch (3 mm) aluminum wire 51 inches (1.3 m) in length and wrap it around the dowel 20 times. Cut another piece, 15 feet (4.6 m) in length, and wrap it 60 times.

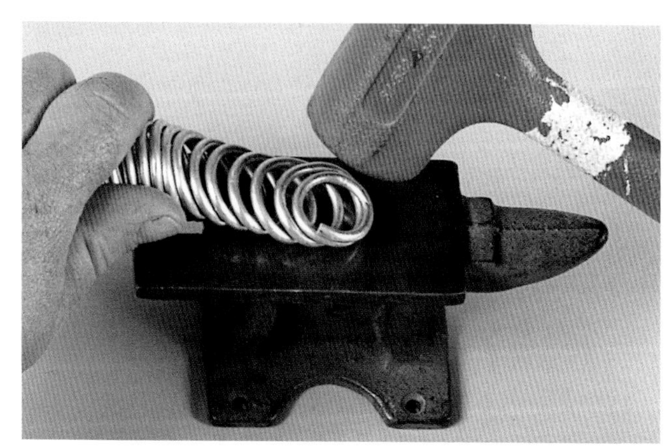

5 With the sand hammer, flatten both coils against the anvil or a smooth piece of steel.

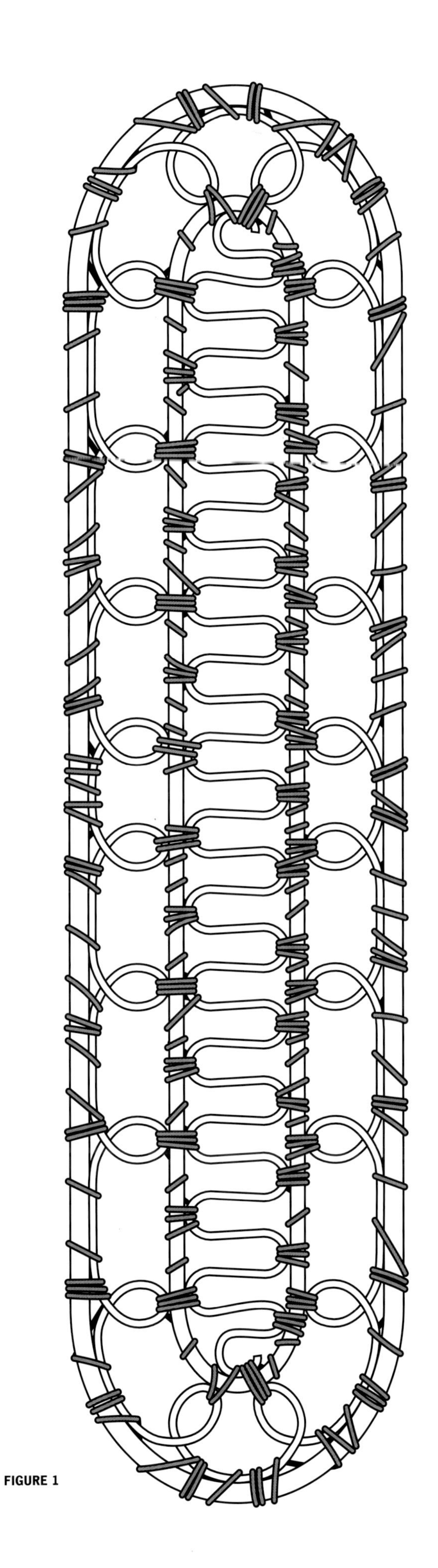

FIGURE 1

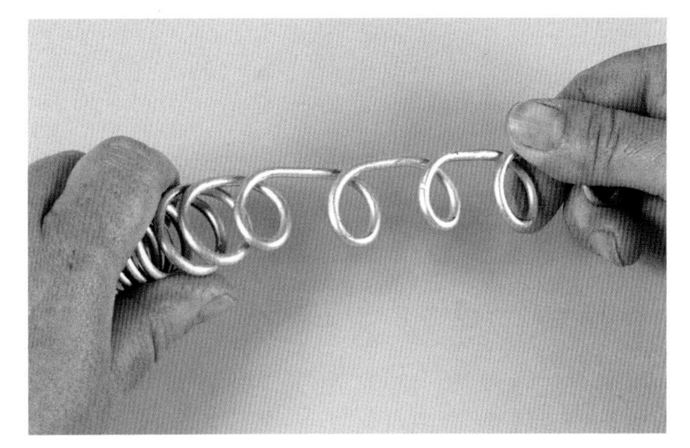

6 Stretch out the coils and adjust them to make sure they will fit on the oval rings. The 20-coil piece will fit around the outer bottom oval. (See figure 1.) The 60-coil piece will fit around the top oval as the decorative rim. (See the detail of the rim in step 11 on page 58.)

Stitching Tips

- Use scrap wire in two or three places to hold the pieces while you work to make the stitching easier.
- Stitch with the 18- or 20-gauge (100 mm or .75 mm) colored wire.
- Start from the inside of the bottom of the basket and work your way out and up.
- Use a simple overcast stitch. When stitching on the loops of the different pieces, make two passes with the wire on each stitch to make it really sturdy. (See figure 1.)

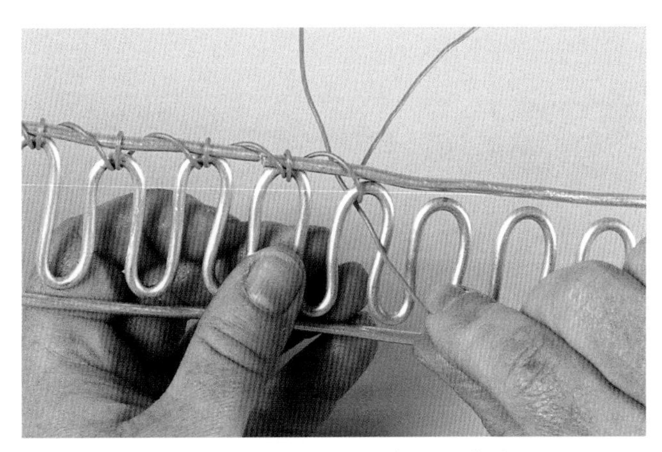

7 Make a few preliminary stitches with the 18- or 20-gauge (1.00 or .75 mm) wire to attach the 17-loop jigged piece to the smaller bottom oval ring. Stretch out and adjust the loops to fit the oval.

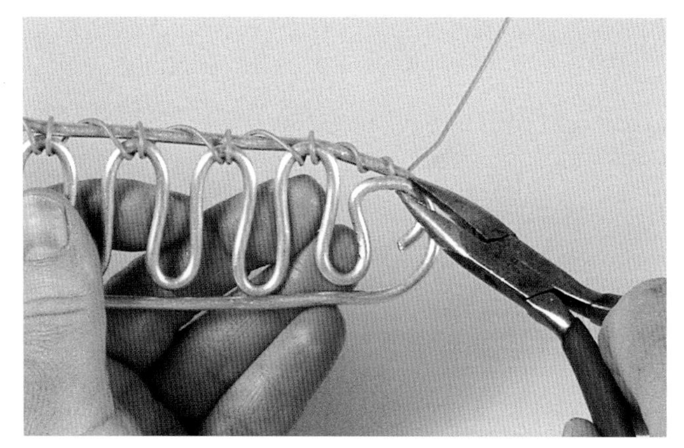

8 With the needle-nose pliers, bend a small curve at each end of the jigged piece to match the curve of the oval.

9 Place the two bottom ovals on the table to make it easier to work. With your fingers, adjust the 20-coil piece between the two ovals. Using figure 1 on the previous page as your guide, stitch the two patterned pieces to the smaller oval ring, catching the loops of both patterned pieces with the same stitch to make a sturdy attachment. Moving outward, stitch the coil piece to the outer bottom oval. You've attached all four pieces and completed the bottom of the basket.

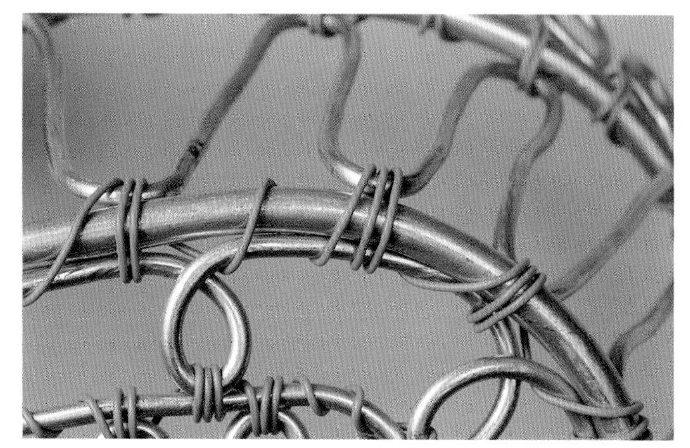

10 To attach the sides: Stitch the bottom bends of the 48-loop jigged side piece to the outer bottom oval ring.

11 To attach the top three pieces: Stitch together the oval ring, the top of the side piece, and the 60-coil decorative rim—catching the loops with the same stitch you used on the bottom section in step 9. With the wire cutters, remove all the scrap wires.

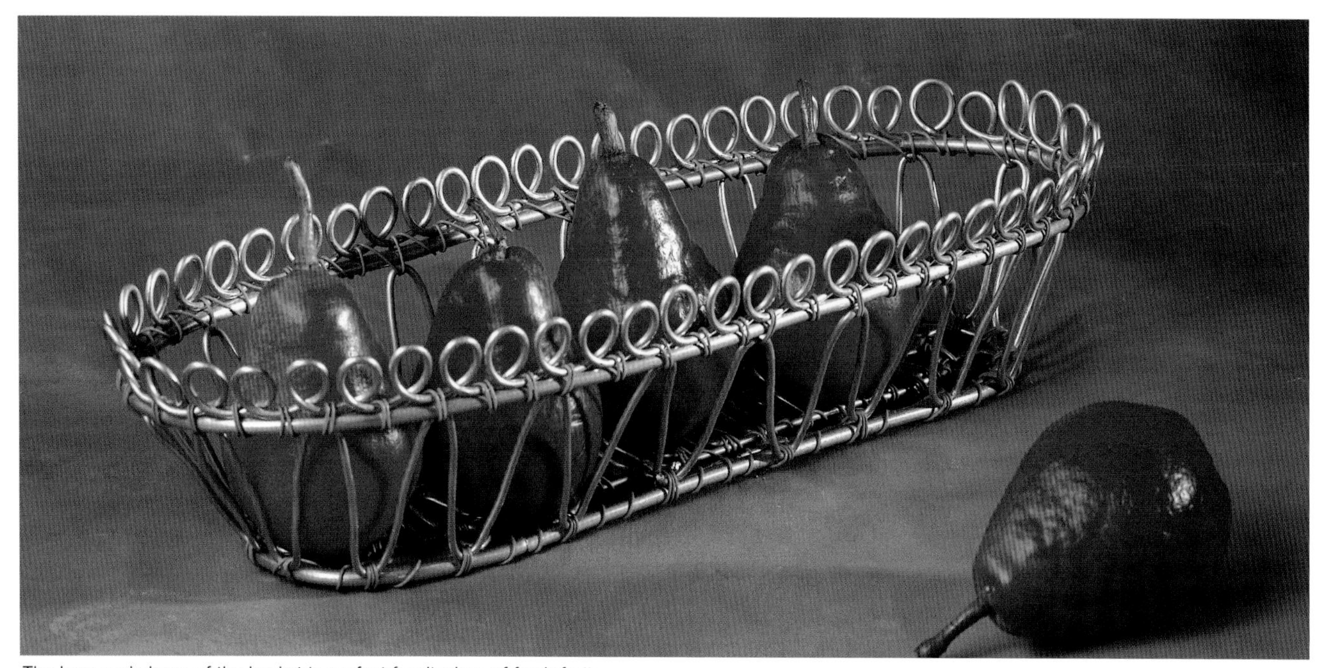

The long oval shape of the basket is perfect for displays of fresh fruit.

Wordy Bookmark

This beautiful bookmark keeps your place on the page in any size book. Formed entirely from just one piece of wire, it takes less than a half-hour to make. Texturing and flattening the wires as the final touch will really make the project read well.

YOU WILL NEED

18- or 20-gauge (1.00 or .75 mm) steel, brass, or copper wire, 30 inches (76.2 cm) in length

Wire cutters

Needle-nose pliers

Round-nose pliers

Slip-joint pliers

Polished steel hammer

Anvil or smooth piece of steel

BEFORE YOU START

Practice with very thin scrap wire, such as 24-gauge (.50 mm), to learn how to form the letters and shapes of your design. To determine how much wire you'll need for the final design, stretch out your practice wire and measure it. Also, see the samples of hammer marks in Wirework Basics on page 22. Remember, never crush wires that cross each other—you'll weaken them, and they'll break where they cross.

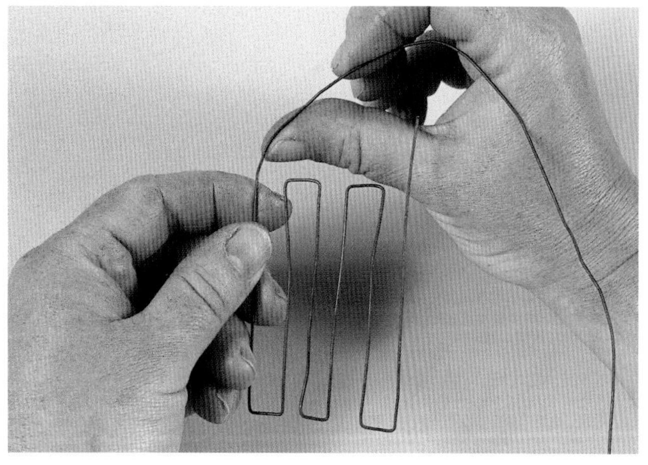

1 With your fingers, bend the wire into the shape of your design.

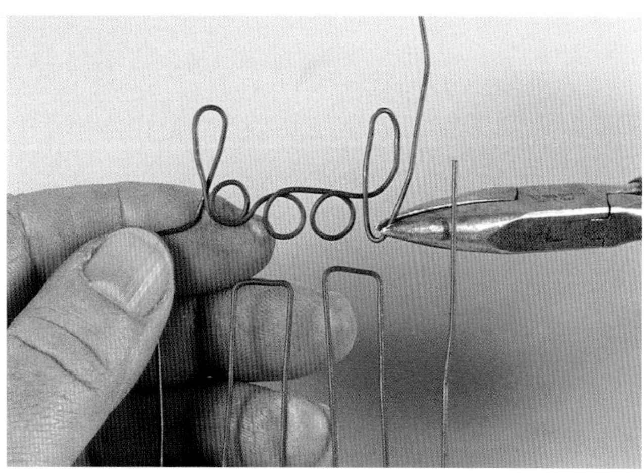

2 You may want to use the needle-nose or the round-nose pliers to help with the smaller details.

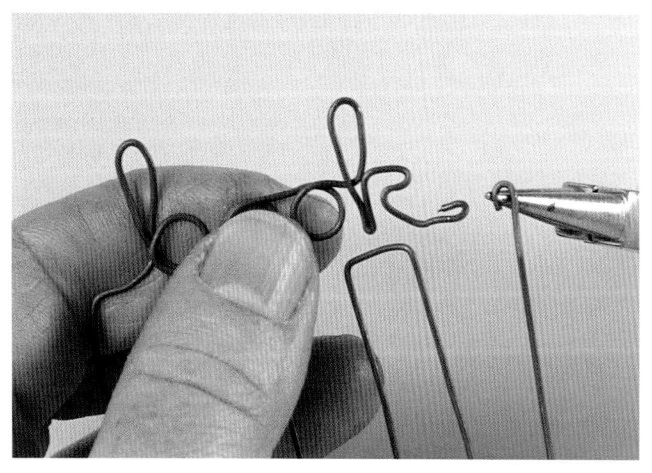

3 Using the round-nose pliers, make tiny hooks at both ends of the wire.

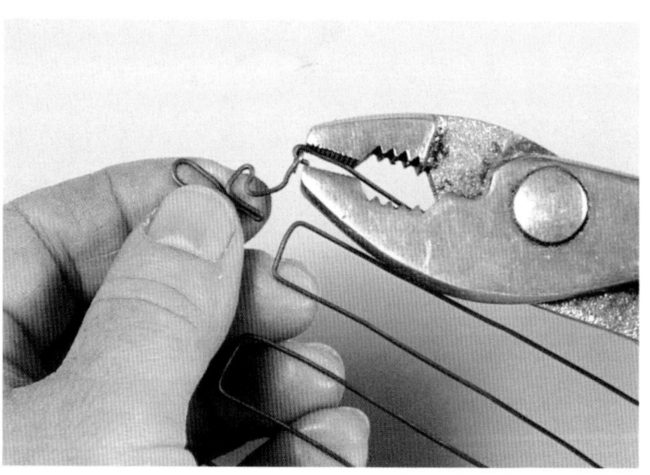

4 With the slip-joint pliers, crimp the hooks together.

5 Use the steel hammer to squish the wire against the anvil or the piece of steel. This will stiffen the wire and help it keep its shape.

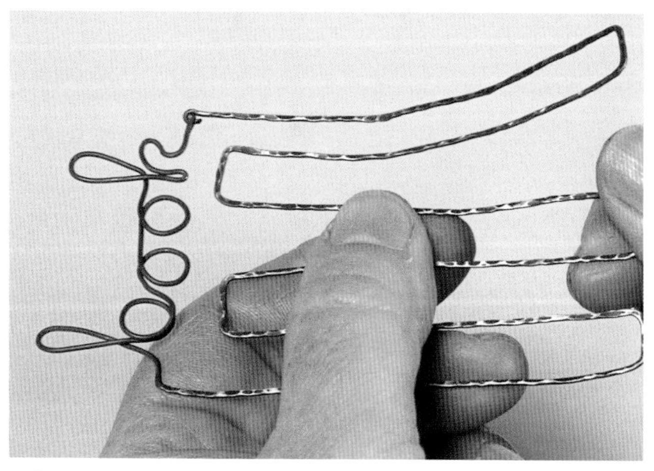

6 With your fingers, re-adjust the hammered shape.

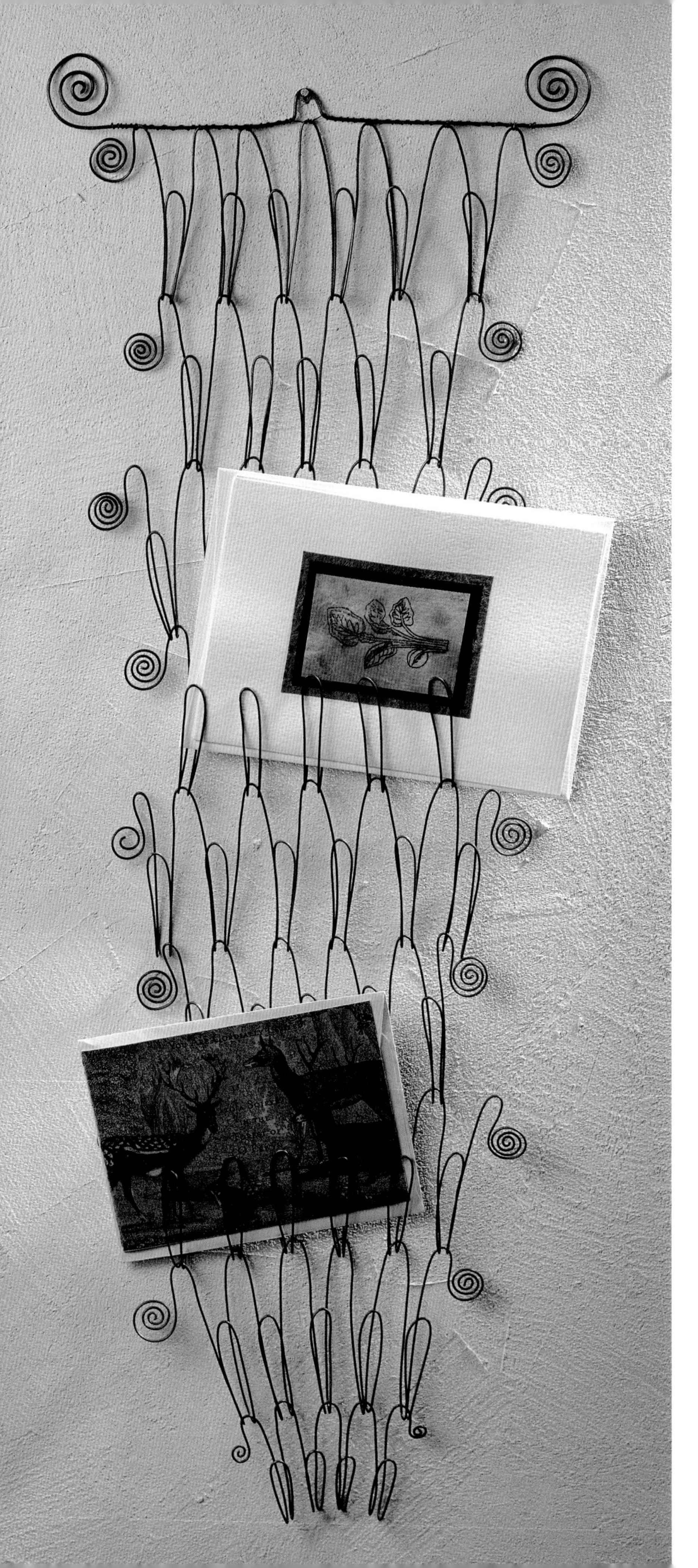

Interlocking Letter Rack

Useful and beautiful, this letter rack keeps important things from getting lost and looks great hanging on the wall above my desk—I love looking at it. The rack can be longer or shorter, depending on how many sections you add on.

YOU WILL NEED

(FOR A 5-SECTION RACK)

18-gauge (1.00 mm) wire, 30 feet (9.1 m) in length

16-gauge (1.25 mm) wire, 20 inches (50.8 cm) in length

24-gauge (.50 mm) wire, 12 inches (30.5 cm) in length

Flat jig, fixed or adjustable

Ruler

China marker or chalk

Wire cutters

Flat-nose pliers

Round-nose pliers

BEFORE YOU START

- The how-to steps describe how to make a rack with 5 sections.
- If you want to make a longer rack, such as the 9-sectioned one in the photo to the left, just increase the number of sections.
- Each section uses about 6 feet (1.8 m) of 18-gauge (1.00 mm) wire, so multiply that by the number of sections you want in your letter rack, to get the total length of wire you'll need.

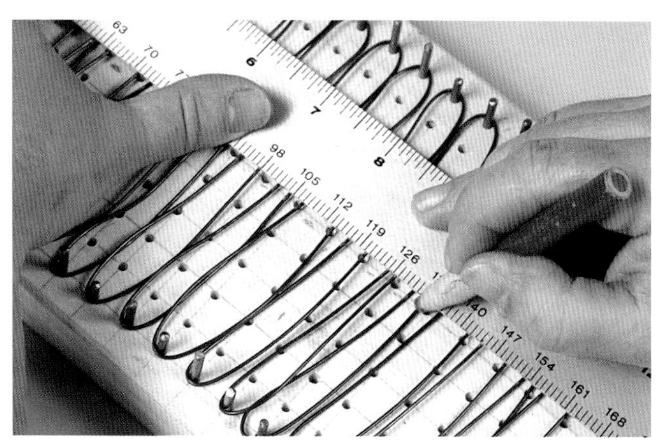

1 To make the sections: Set the jig at intervals of $^{1}/_{2}$ x 5 inches (1.3 x 12.7 cm). Bend the 18-gauge (1.00 mm) wire 28 times around the nails. Before you take the wire off the jig, use the ruler and the china marker or chalk to measure and mark a line across all the wires 3 inches (7.6 cm) from the top of the jig. You will bend the wires at this mark in step 3.

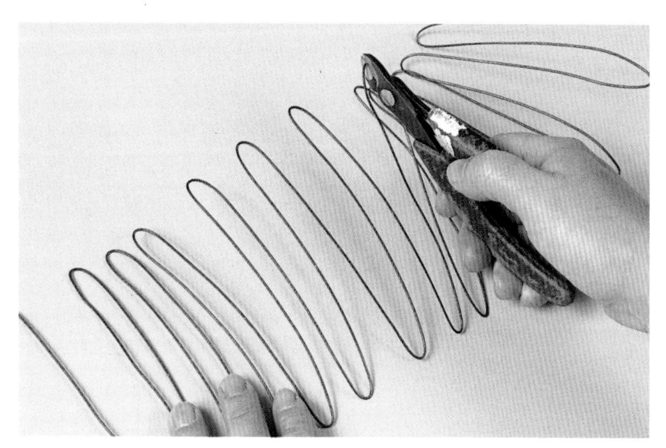

2 Counting the bottom loops of the pattern, use the wire cutters to cut three pieces with six full loops each. Then cut two more pieces with five full loops on the bottom.

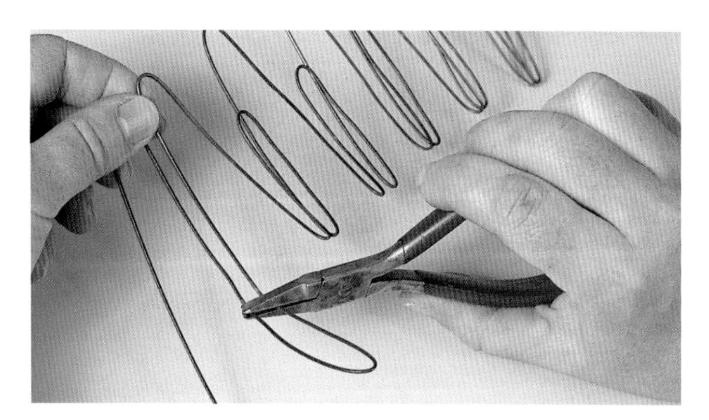

3 Using the flat-nose pliers and your fingers, bend the loops of all five pieces in half at the 3-inch (7.6 cm) mark you made in step 1.

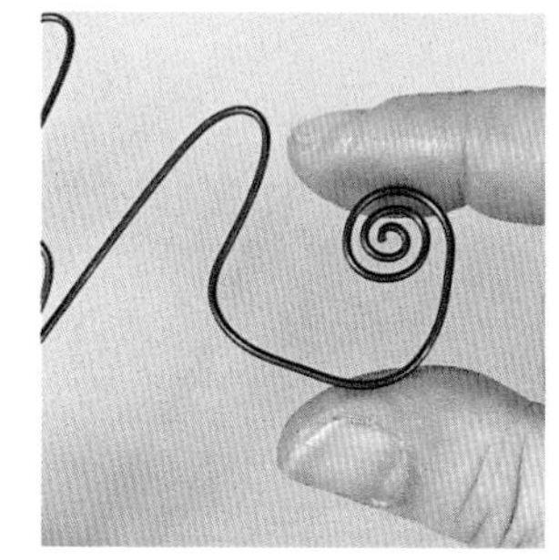

4 Each piece will have a long wire remaining at either side on the bottom—you'll use these to make the spirals. Start the spirals using the round-nose pliers. Continue spiraling with your fingers or the flat-nose pliers.

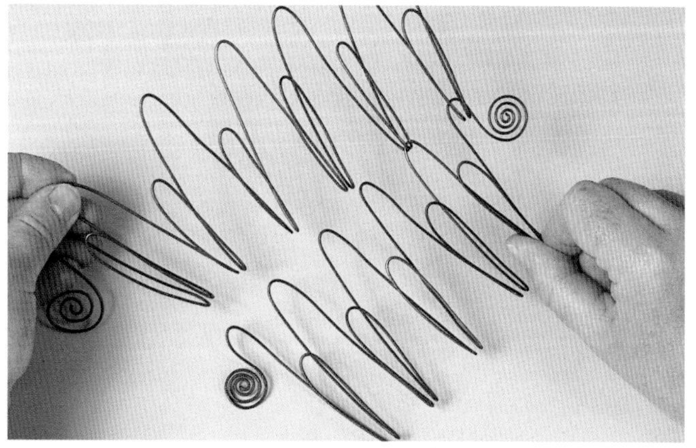

5 To make all the patterns even, straighten out each piece with your fingers. Then, working from bottom to top, link the five pieces together. The bottom piece is one of the 6-loop pieces. Link its top with the bottom of a piece with 5 loops. Then link the top of that 5-loop piece with the bottom of the second 6-loop piece. Finally, link the second 5-loop and the third 6-loop pieces.

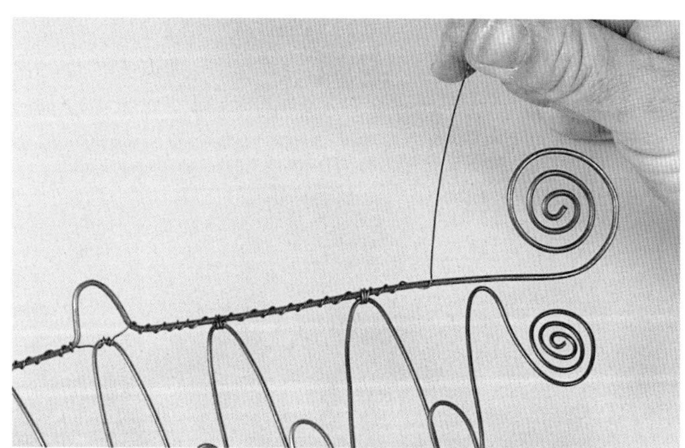

6 To make the piece at the top for hanging: Curl both ends of the 16-gauge (1.25 mm) wire into spirals. (See step 4.) Then, use your fingers to make a bend in the center of the wire for hanging. With the 24-gauge (.50 mm) wire, stitch the piece onto the top loops of the last 6-loop section.

Sassy Salad Set

I have made a lot of these salad sets, and people just love them. They work great and look wonderful hanging on a wall. Use tins of different colors for a variety of looks.

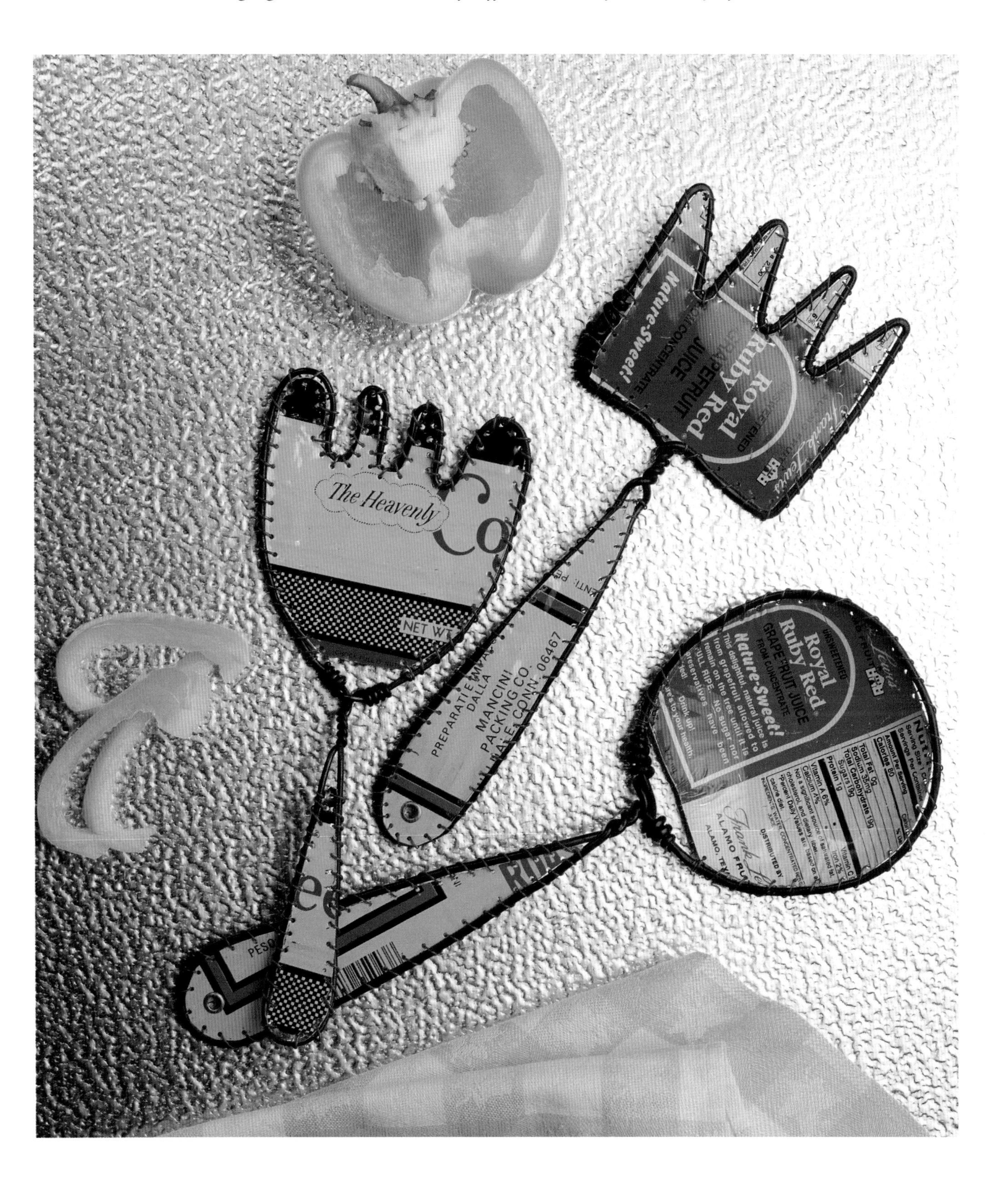

YOU WILL NEED

12-gauge (2.00 mm) steel or brass wire, 56 inches (1.4 m) in length

24- or 26-gauge (.50 mm or .41 mm) colored wire, 4 feet (1.22 m) in length

Tin can with printed design

Tape measure

Wire cutters

Vise

Vise grip pliers

Flat-nose pliers

File or emery board

Sharp nail or stylus

Regular household scissors (Don't use your best pair.)

Gloves

A piece of scrap wood

Hammer

Sharp nail for punching holes

Wide masking tape or clear packing tape

Phone book

Wooden pestle or baseball bat

BEFORE YOU START

Practice on thin scrap wire to learn how to bend the fork and spoon frames and to determine how much wire you'll need for your design.

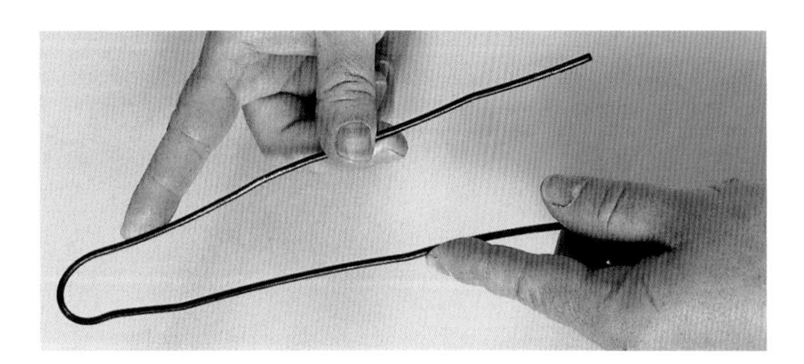

1 To make the handles: Using the tape measure and wire cutters, measure and cut two pieces of 12-gauge (2.00 mm) wire: one 26 inches (66 cm) long for the spoon; and the other 30 inches (76.2 cm) long for the fork. Bend each piece of wire 8 inches (20.3 cm) from one end.

2 Clamp 4 inches (10.2 cm) of each looped end into the vise. With the vise grip pliers, twist the exposed wire closest to the vise three or four times.

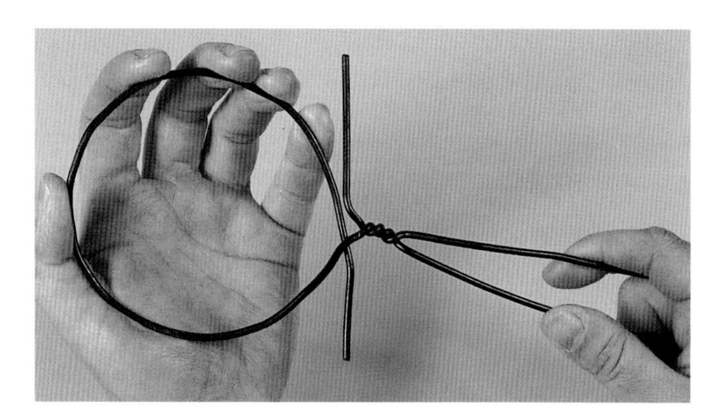

3 To make the shapes of the frames: Bend the long ends of one of the wires into the shape of the spoon. Use the flat-nose pliers, if necessary. Repeat to make the shape of the fork.

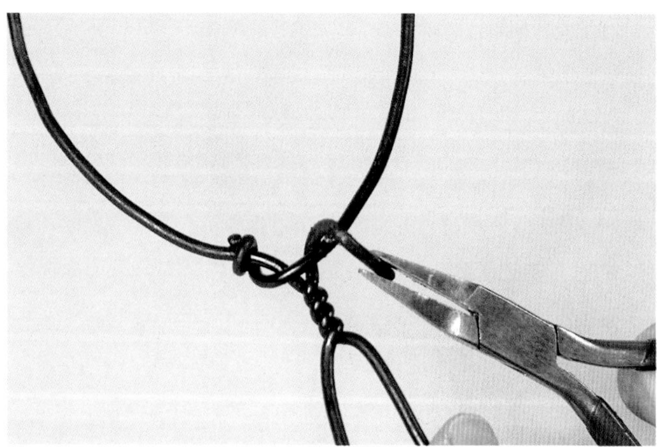

4 File or sand the ends of the wires to make them neat. Using flat-nose pliers, bend the ends to tuck them out of the way and give them a more finished look.

5 To make the tin insides of the fork: With the sharp nail or stylus, trace the shapes of your fork design and its handle on a flattened tin can. Wear gloves, and with the scissors, cut out the shape.

6 Place the tin shapes on a piece of scrap wood and use the hammer and the sharp nail or stylus to punch tiny stitching holes around the perimeters of both tin shapes. Make sure to file off the metal burrs left around the holes from the punching process.

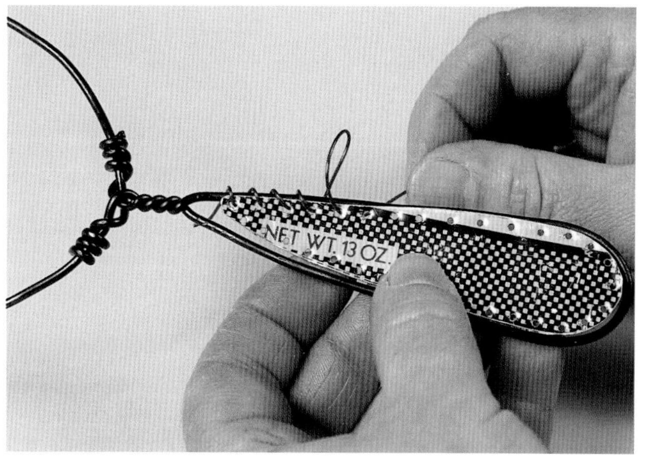

7 With the colored wire, stitch through the holes in each tin shape to connect it to the wire frame.

8 To make the tin insides of the spoon: Repeat steps 5 and 6. To give the spoon its round bowl, you need to mold it a bit. First, protect the tin with tape—either wide masking tape or clear packing tape, then place it on an open phone book. Use a piece of wood with a rounded end, such as a pestle or the end of a baseball bat, to pound the bowl shape. Then, as you did in step 7 for the fork, stitch the tin bowl shapes to the frame.

CARE TIPS

If you use the utensils regularly, remember to wash them with mild detergent, and don't scrub them too hard. The paint layer on tin is scratched easily. I also recommend oiling them with olive oil after each use to keep the rust away.

Flying Fish Mobile

This colorful project is an excellent way to "draw" on your imagination. Making a mobile means making a lot of parts—in different sizes, different colors, and different weights—so you have a lot of choices. Balance is the real challenge of this project. Try one element, then another, and let gravity and a gentle breeze help you achieve the final look.

YOU WILL NEED

24-, 14-, and 12-gauge (.50, 1.50, and 2.00 mm) wire, brass, copper, steel, and colored
Wire cutters
Flat-nose pliers
Round-nose pliers

BEFORE YOU START

The frames should be made with 14- or 12-gauge (1.50 or 2.00 mm) wire, which is strong enough to support the elements hanging from it. The vertical suspension wires can be made with 24-gauge (.50 mm) wire.

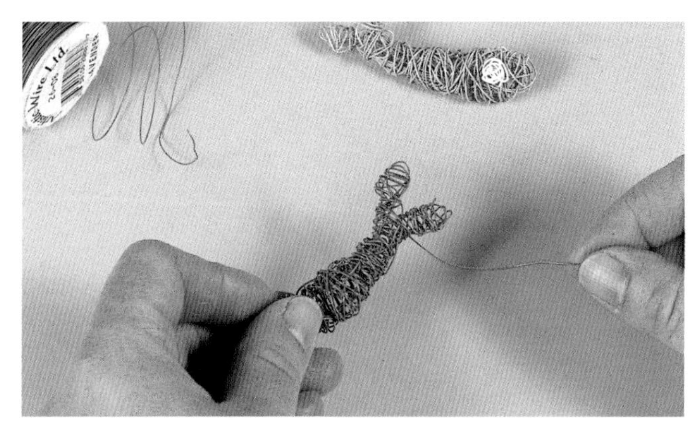

1 Make lots of hanging fish in different sizes and shapes and from any gauge wire you want. Just bend a wire (any wire) into a basic fish shape and then wrap wire around it to build up a shape you like.

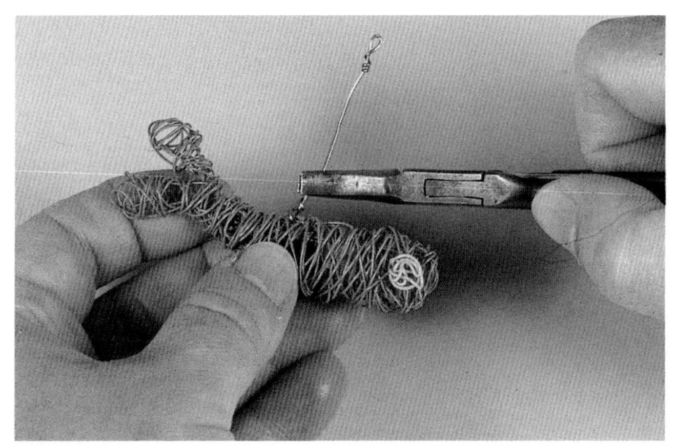

2 Cut different lengths of 24-gauge (.50 mm) wire to make the vertical suspension wires. Hook these to the fish shapes. Twist the hooks closed with flat-nose pliers.

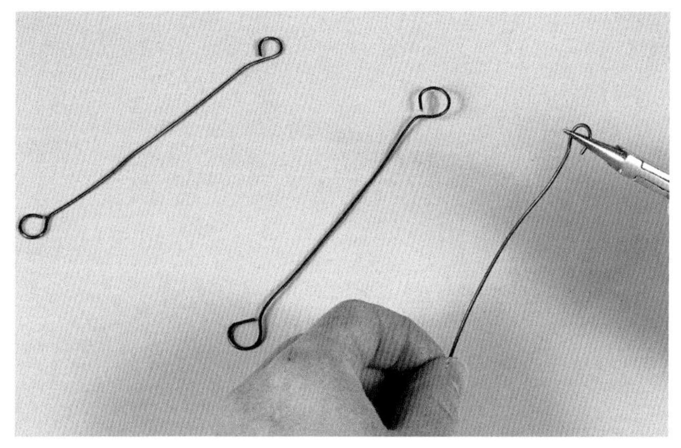

3 Make several horizontal wire frames in various lengths and gauge sizes. Also make a few vertical suspension wires to vary the design and movement. Use round-nose pliers to make hooks on both ends of both the wire frames and the suspension wires.

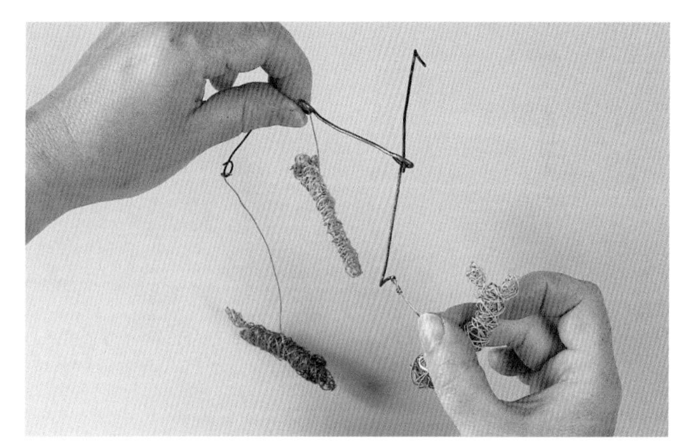

4 Gradually attach and assemble the hanging fish shapes, suspension wires, frames, and extenders until everything balances.

Different colored wires add variety to the fish shapes.

Coiled Wire Basket

Believe it or not, this basket is the first project I teach students in my wire workshop. It's challenging only the first time you go through the steps. Then a whole world opens up, and you can make baskets in any shape and size you want.

YOU WILL NEED

25 mm) steel wire, 10 feet (3 m) in length

57 mm) steel wire, 10 feet (3 m) in length

0 mm) steel wire, 30 feet (9.1 m) in length

Paper

Pencil

Wire cutters

Masking tape

Slip-joint pliers

Flat-nose pliers

BEFORE YOU START

Make the rim circle by twisting 20 inches (50.8 cm) of 16-gauge (1.25 mm) wire to a length of 10 inches (25.4 cm). (See the twisting section in Wirework Basics on page 21.) The basket shown is 5 inches (12.7 cm) tall. Adjust the sizes and lengths of wire to be compatible with the size of your basket.

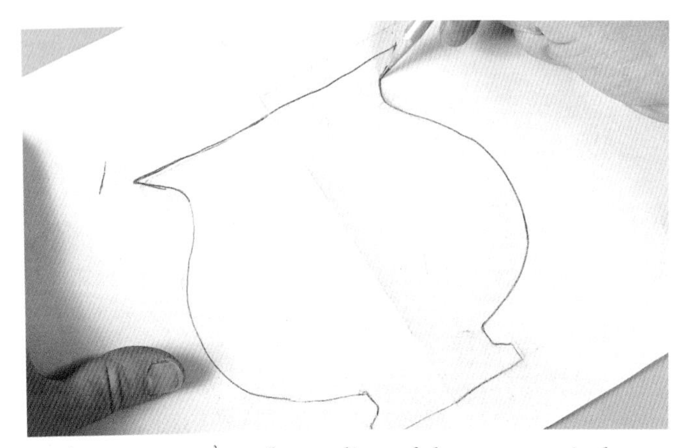

1 Draw on paper the outline of the symmetrical basket. Use the template below, or make one of your own.

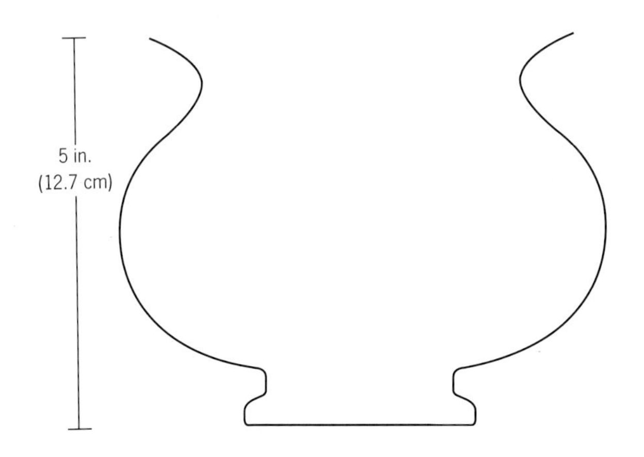

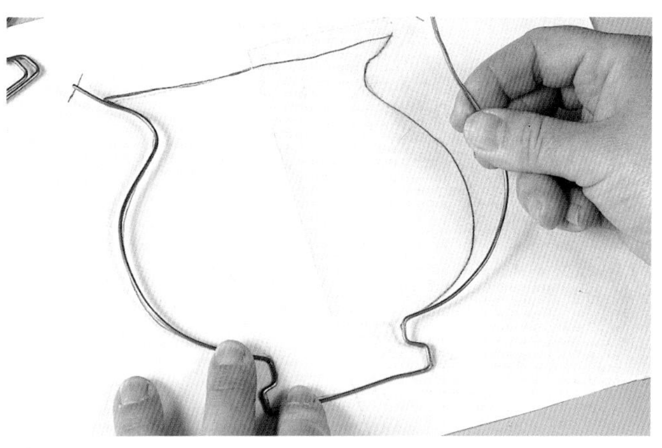

2 To make the six ribs of the basket: You need three wire tracings of the basket's shape. Bend three pieces of the 16-gauge (1.25 mm) wire along the outlines of the basket you drew on paper. As you do this, turn the paper instead of the wire, and the wire will be easier to shape. Be sure to leave 1/2 inch (1.3 cm) of extra wire at the top of all the ends, then cut.

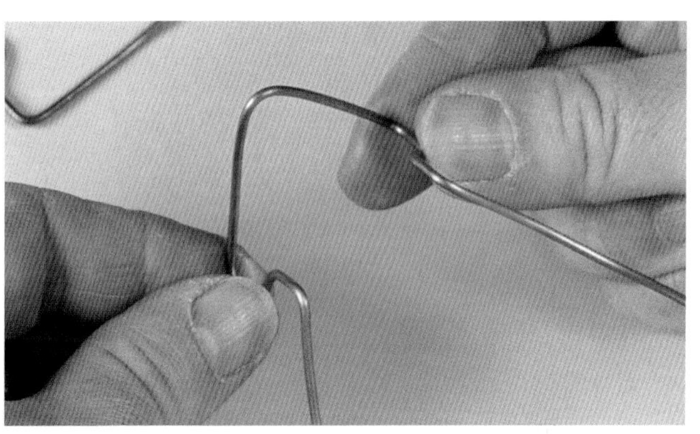

3 At the center bottom of each bent piece of wire, make a 45° bend. This will keep the wires firmly in place so they won't slide around.

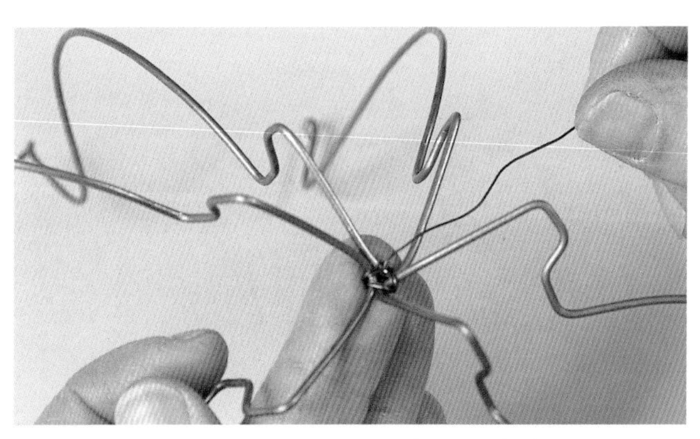

4 Tie all three bent wires together with the 23-gauge (.57 mm) wire. (Be sure to tuck in the little wire ends, so they don't poke out.)

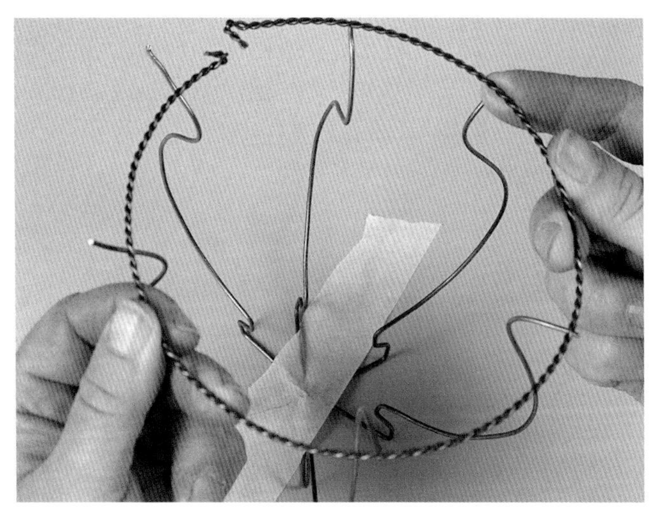

5 To make the rim of the basket: Shape the 10-inch (25.4 cm) piece of twisted 16-gauge (1.25 mm) wire into the rim circle. Use the masking tape to hold the bottoms of the ribs to the tabletop, so you can work with them easily. Bend hooks on both ends of the circle and crimp them together with the slip-joint pliers.

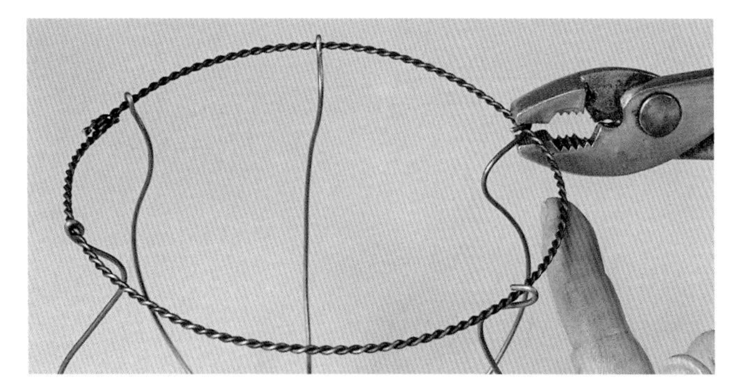

6 To attach the ribs to the rim circle: With flat-nose pliers, make a hook on the end of each of the six rib wires. With the slip-joint pliers, squeeze these hooks tightly onto the rim.

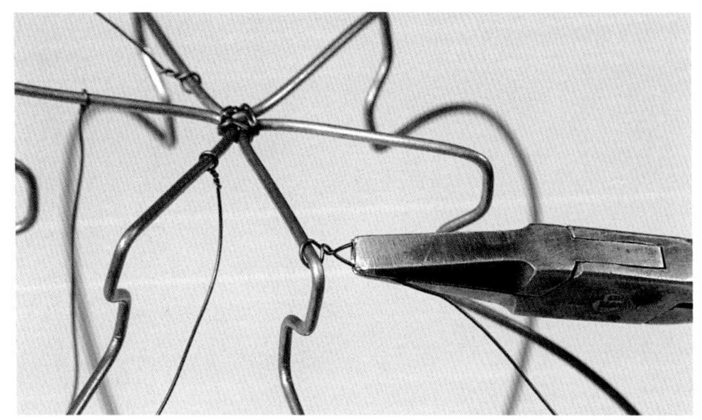

7 Cut six pieces of the 23-gauge (.57 mm) wire, each 2 feet (61 cm) long. With flat-nose pliers, tie each one of these wires to the bottom of each of the six ribs, close to where you joined the six ribs together in step 4.

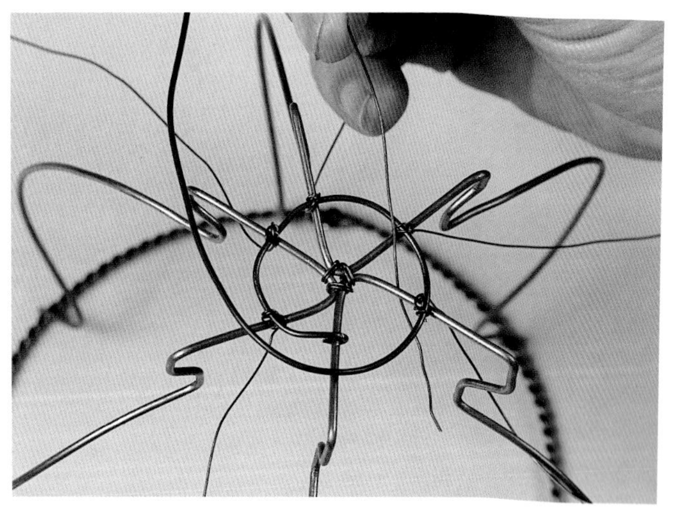

8 To make the sides of the basket: With the flat-nose pliers, make a small hook at the end of the 30-foot length (9.1 m) of 18-gauge (1.00 mm) wire. Attach the wire to the bottom of one of the ribs by crimping the hook closed with the slip-joint pliers. Coil the free end of the 18-gauge (1.00 mm) wire around the basket ribs, starting at the bottom. Each time the coiling wire passes a rib, wrap it with the 23-gauge (.57 mm) wire that you tied onto that rib.

9 Continue coiling, working your way to the top, until you reach the rim of the basket.

10 If you're consistent with your coiling, a pattern will gradually develop. For a decorative effect, you may space the coils closely at the widest portion of the basket. Make a hook at the end of the coiling wire and crimp it to the rib where it ends. Tie off and tuck in all the wrapping wire.

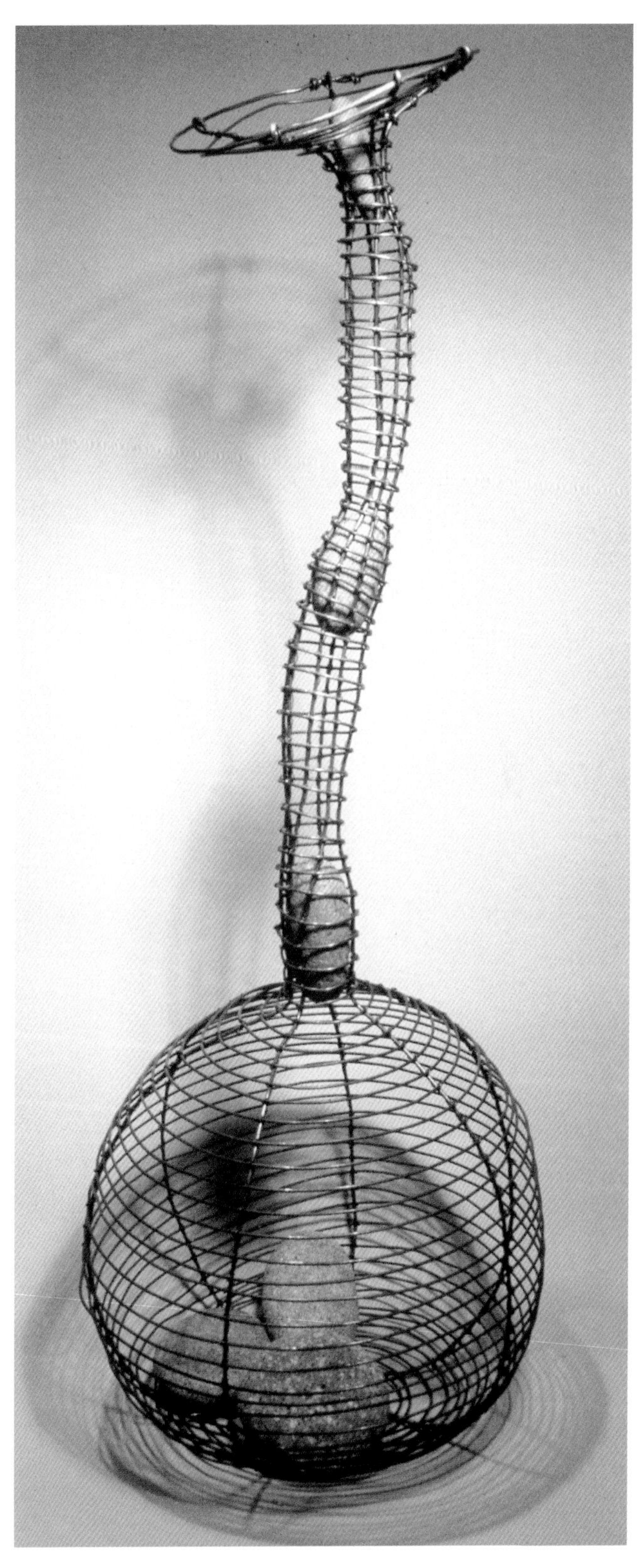

Above: Ellen Wieske, Swallowing Basket, 1996, steel wire and beach stones, 3 x 1 ft. (91.4 x 30.5 cm), photo by artist

Left: Ellen Wieske, Vase with Flowers, steel wire, 20 x 7 in. (50.8 x 17.8 cm), photo by artist

Jason Kelty, *Woody Wire*, 1999, steel wire, 10 x 5 x 5 in. (25.4 x 12.7 x 12.7 cm), photo by Bob Payne

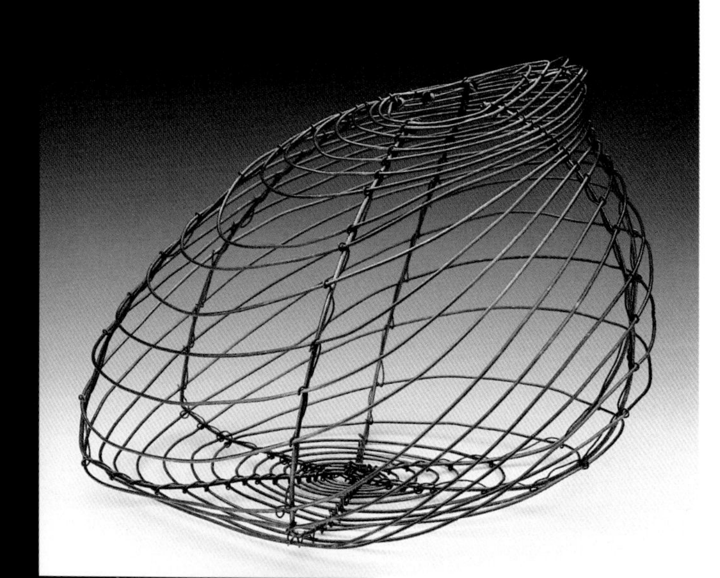

Jason Kelty, *Seedy Wire*, 1999, steel wire, 8 x 10 x 10 in. (20.3 x 25.4 x 25.4 cm), photo by Bob Payne

Ellen Wieske, *Magazine Rack,* 1999, steel wire, 18 x 14 x 8 in. (45.7 x 35.6 x 20.3 cm), photo by artist

Kathleen Bolan, *Basket Case*, 2000, sterling silver wire and silver Bali beads, 5 x 3 in. (12.7 x 7.6 cm), including handle, photo by Tim Thayer

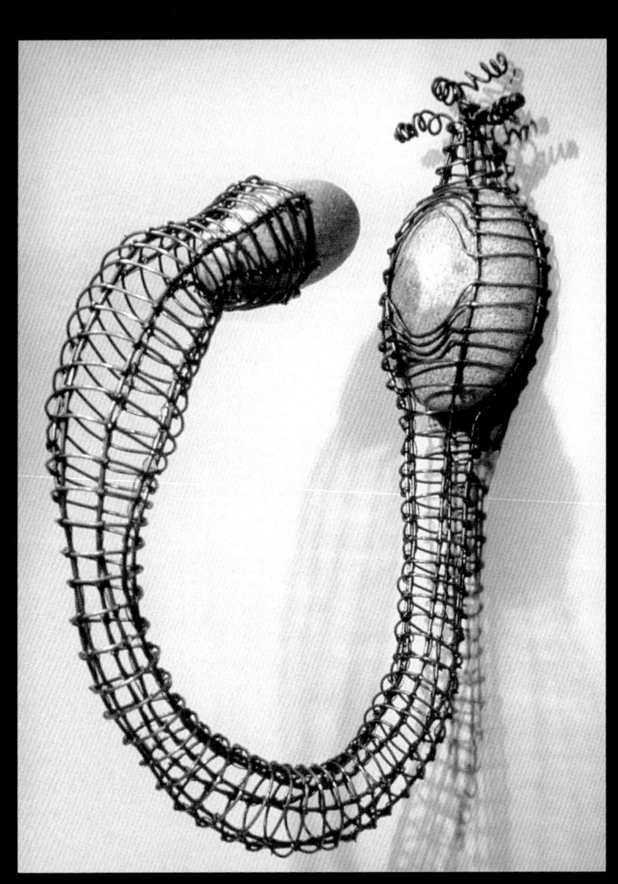

Ellen Wieske, *Door Knocker*, 1996, steel wire and beach stones, 14 in. (35.6 cm), photo by artist

Ingrid Menken, *Pitcher,* 1995, steel wire, 13 x 7 in. (33 x 17.8 cm), photo by Evan Bracken

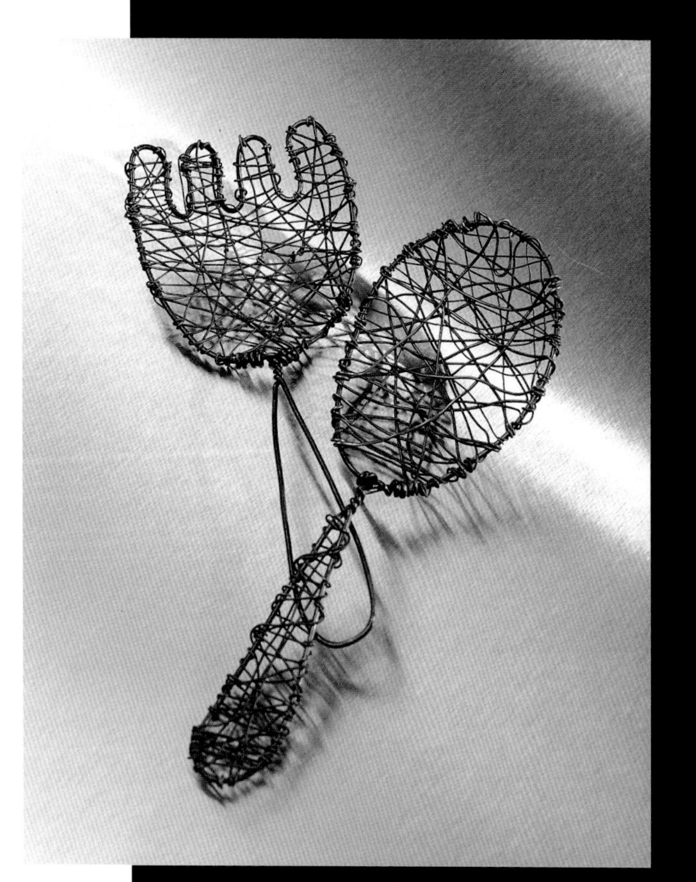

Ellen Wieske, *Salad Set,* 1999, steel wire, $7^1/_2$ x 3 in. (19.1 x 7.6 cm), photo by Evan Bracken

Ellen Wieske, *Vase,* 2000, steel wire, 7 x $4^1/_2$ (17.8 x 11.4 cm), photo by Evan Bracken

Ellen Wieske/Carole Ann Fer, *Plate,* 2000, porcelain, steel wire, $5^1/_2$ in. diameter (14 cm), photo by Evan Bracken

Nancy Nicholson, *Wire Hat,* 1999, steel and brass wire, 3 x 12 in. (7.6 x 30.5 cm), photo by Evan Bracken

Nancy Nicholson, *Bowl,* 1999, steel wire and parts, 6 x 8 in. (15.2 x 20.3 cm), photo by Evan Bracken

Ellen Wieske, *Untitled,* 1999, steel wire, 7 1/2 in. (19.1 cm), photo by Evan Bracken

Susan Rankin, *Blue Bottle,* 1999, blown glass, steel wire, $8^1/_2$ x 12 x 6 in. (21.6 x 30.5 x 15.2 cm), photo by artist

Priscilla Turner Spada, *Bittersweet,* 1999, neckpiece and earrings of handmade lampworked glass beads, sterling silver and copper wire, $6^1/_2$ x 6 x $^1/_2$ in. (16.5 x 15.2 x 1.3 cm), photo by Pierre Chiha

Susan Rankin, *Wire Form # 1,* 1998, blown glass, steel wire, $11^1/_2$ x 12 in. (29.2 x 30.5 cm), photo by Michael Callen

Reg Logan, *U-Swat-'Em Flyswatter,* 1999, steel wire, used tin can, lampworked glass beads, 14 x 4 in. (35.6 x 10.2. cm), photo, Evan Bracken # 495

Solveig Cox, *Wire Cat,* 1999, steel wire, 7 x 8 in. (17.8 x 20.3 cm), photo by Evan Bracken

Reg Logan, *Homage Pour Anchois,* 1999, steel wire with used French anchovy tin, $6^{1}/_{2}$ x 5 in. (16.5 x 12.7 cm), photo by Evan Bracken

Ellen Wieske, *Brooch*, 1998, steel wire, $1^1/_2$ x 3 in. (3.8 cm x 7.6 cm), photo by artist

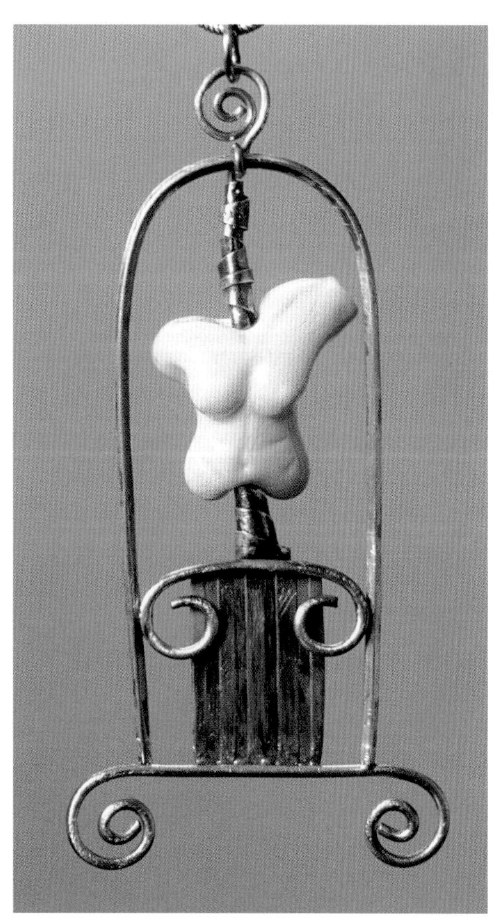

Priscilla Turner Spada, *Classical Torso Pendant*, 2000, handmade lampworked glass bead, sterling silver wire, 2 x $1^1/_2$ x $^1/_2$ in. (5.1 x 3.8 x 1.3 cm), photo by Pierre Chiha

Jennifer Cornwell, *Blue Tide*, 1999, wire goblet with glass beads, 7 x $3^1/_2$ in. (17.8 x 8.9 cm), photo by Evan Bracken,

Priscilla Turner Spada, *Victorian Pendant,* 1998, cast glass, steel wire, $1^3/_4$ x $1^1/_2$ x $^5/_8$ in. (4.4 x 3.8 x 1.6 cm), photo by Pierrre Chiha

Kathleen Bolan, *Grandma's Perm,* 2000, sterling silver wire bracelet, 8 in. (20.3 cm), photo by Tim Thayer

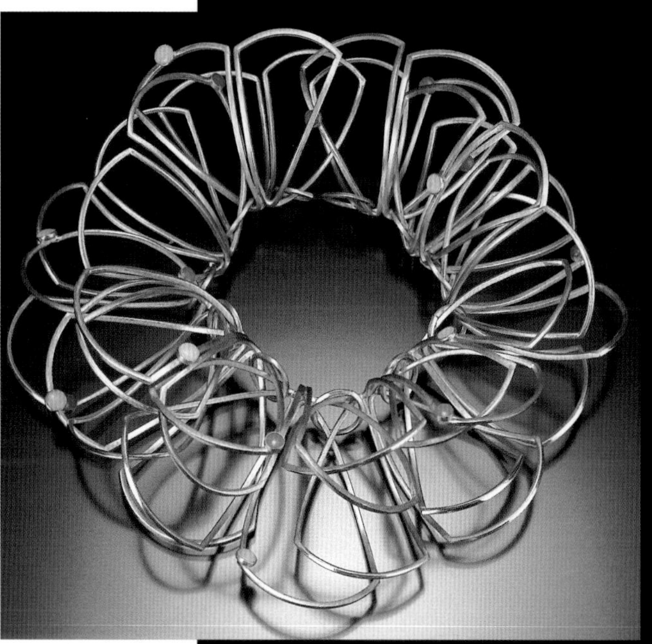

Anne Mondro, *Untitled,* 1999, bracelet of sterling silver wire, opals, epoxy resins, 2 x 6 x $1\frac{1}{2}$ in. (5.1 x 15.2 x 3.8 cm), photo by Robert Diamante

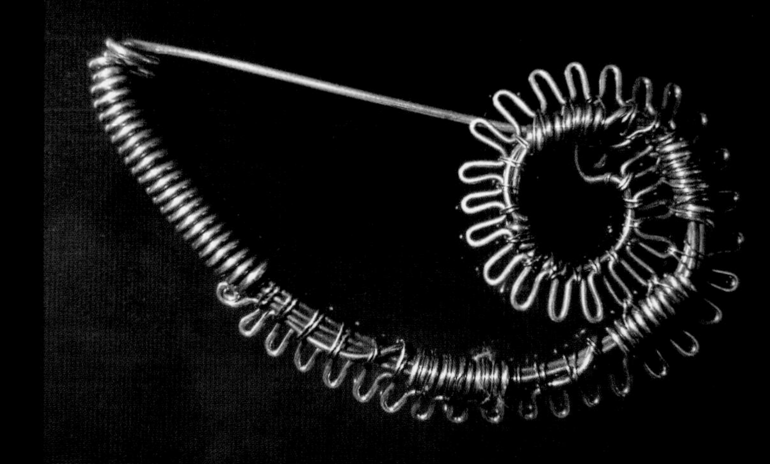

Ellen Wieske, *Brooch,* 1998, sterling silver and steel wire, $2\frac{1}{2}$ x $4\frac{1}{2}$ in. (6.4 x 11.4 cm), photo by artist

Acknowledgments

When I was approached by Deborah Morgenthal from Lark Books to write a book on working with wire, I had no idea just what to expect. I know how to make things. I thought I knew how to explain how to make things. Thank you to everyone at Lark who held my hand every step of the way. You helped make my dream of producing this book come true. You are a talented and gracious bunch. Thank you, Deborah, for taking the chance on me. To my editor, Marcianne Miller—a patient, kind and professional wordsmith—thank you. Your enthusiasm and direction were instrumental in getting this done. Thank you to the talented eyes of photographers Richard Hasselberg, who shot the instructional photos, and Evan Bracken, who photographed the projects. Thank you to art directors Celia Naranjo and Tom Metcalf, whose clear vision pulled everything together and made each page look perfect. A special thanks to everyone who contributed work for the gallery sections. Your works in wire are an inspiration to all, especially me. I am thrilled and honored to be lucky enough to be able to include your work. Last, but not least, thank you to my family and friends for listening and for being so supportive. The kind of help you gave cannot be overestimated. Thank you, Carole Ann. Thank you, Dad, for teaching me how to use tools and to love making things.

Contributing Artists

KATHLEEN BOLAN makes her own lampworked glass beads and creates wire jewelry which she sells at fine art shows and in select galleries. Her company is Born to Bead, in Trenton, Michigan.

CHRISTINE CLARK is a sculptor who works primarily in steel and steel wire, as well as with a variety of mixed materials, including cement, wood and hair. She teaches at Oregon College of Art and Craft, in Portland, Oregon.

JENNIFER CORNWELL, artist, art therapist, and educator, teaches and facilitates workshops throughout New England.

SOLVEIG COX is a Virginia potter who makes pottery about cats. She took a class with Ellen Wieske and now she is making wire pieces about cats.

DONNA D'AQUINO teaches jewelry and metalsmithing at the University of Akron, in Akron, Ohio.

CAROLE ANN FER is a studio potter and teaches in New England. She makes functional pots and collaborates with Ellen Wieske on wire and clay pieces.

JASON KELTY, a Shepherdsville, Kentucky artist, draws from nature, creating organic forms in a variety of manufactured media.

REG LOGAN is a New Hampshire glass and metal artist fascinated with insects and their ability to survive and adapt through time. She exhibits in galleries in the U.S. and France.

ANNE MONDRO is a graduate student pursuing her MFA at Kent State University, in Kent, Ohio.

INGRID MENKEN works as a jeweler, printmaker, and mixed media artist in Maine. She creates wire baskets for friends and family.

NANCY NICHOLSON worked as a stained glass artist for 15 years in the Boston area. After studying jewelry-making and wirework with Ellen Wieske, she's added a new passion to her art—wire.

SUSAN RANKIN is a glassblower who is currently working on a series of works combining glass and wire forms. She lives in Ontario, Canada.

PRISCILLA TURNER SPADA, a glass bead and jewelry artist, uses a variety of metalsmithing and lampworking techniques to express her love of color, nature and history through her work. She lives in Newburyport, Massachusetts.

KRISTIANA TRÖW SPAULDING is a bi-coastal metal artist whose work is inspired by her travels to Latin America. She lives in San Francisco, California.

About the Author

ELLEN WIESKE has been working as a metalsmith for 24 years and teaching her craft for the past 13. She has taught classes and workshops at colleges, museums, and craft schools throughout the United States, as well as in France. She received her BA from Wayne State University, Detroit, Michigan (1981) and her MFA from Cranbrook Academy of Art, Bloomfield Hills, Michigan (1992). Her work has been exhibited both nationally and internationally, and can be seen in such publications as *The Fine Art of the Tin Can* (Lark Books, 1996), *Spectacles* (Chronicle Books, 1996), "Exhibition in Print 1998" (*Metalsmith* magazine, 1998), *The Artful Teapot* (Thames and Hudson, 2001). Her work can also be seen in many galleries throughout the country. Ellen currently lives and makes art in her new studio, on Deer Isle, in Maine.

Index